W9-ABE-392

WITH

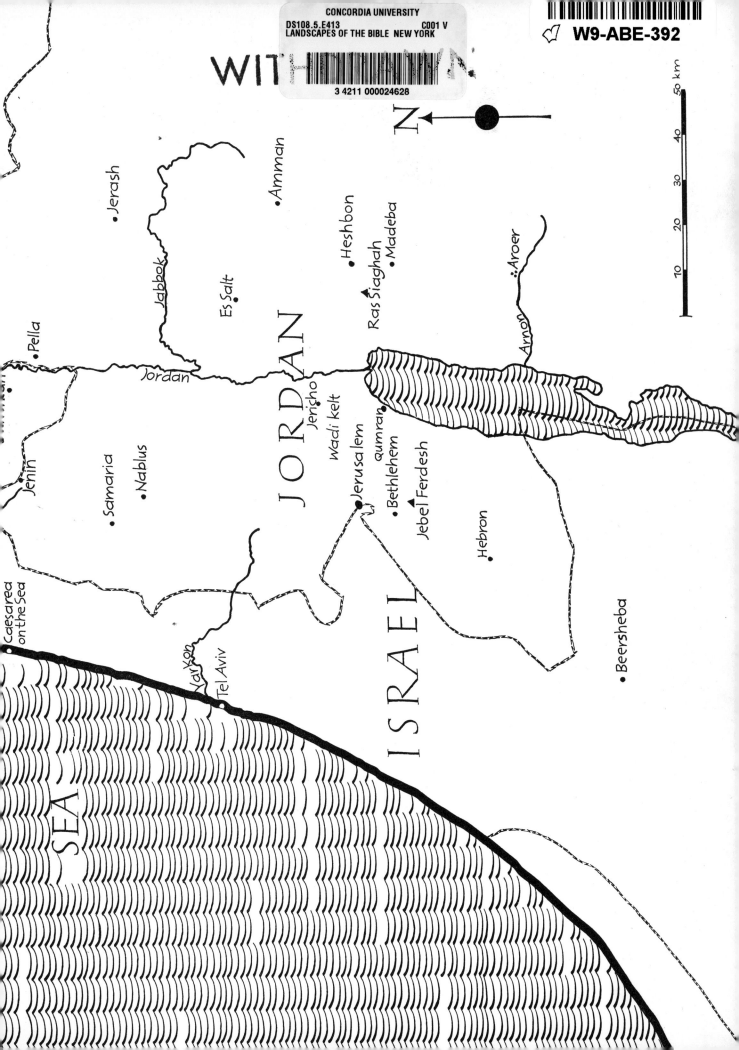

N

50 km
40
30
20
10

Jerash

Amman

Jabbok

Heshbon

Es Salt

Ras Siaghah

Madeba

Aroer

Pella

JORDAN

Jordan

Jericho

Arnon

Wadi kelt

Jenin

Samaria

Nablus

Jerusalem

Qumran

Bethlehem

Jebel Ferdesh

Hebron

J O R D A N

Caesarea
on the Sea

I S R A E L

Yarkon

Tel Aviv

Beersheba

S E A

LANDSCAPES OF THE BIBLE

GEORG EICHHOLZ

LANDSCAPES OF THE BIBLE

TRANSLATED BY JOHN W. DOBERSTEIN

HARPER & ROW · PUBLISHERS
NEW YORK, EVANSTON, AND LONDON

LANDSCAPES OF THE BIBLE – Published in German as LANDSCHAFTEN DER BIBEL
Copyright by Neukirchener Verlag des Erziehungsvereins GmbH, Neukirchen-Vluyn

Library of Congress catalog card number: 63-16402

Reproductions: Carl Schütte & C. Behling, Berlin-Tempelhof. Color: Zeller & Gmelin, Eislingen/Fils. Type: Linotype Futura
Paper: Papierfabrik Scheufelen KG, Oberlenningen/Württ. Jacket, binding, and endpapers designed by Kurt Wolff, Kaiserswerth
Typography, setting, printing, and binding: Breklumer Druckerei Manfred Siegel, Breklum/Schleswig. Printed in West Germany for
Harper and Row, Publishers, Incorporated.

PREFACE

Anyone who picks up this book is in for some surprises. For anyone who has been familiar with the stories of the Bible from childhood will have certain pictures in his mind, pictures of countrysides and cities, scenes and human figures. When we heard or read the stories of the Bible, how could we help but picture the places where they occurred? Did we not imagine, for example, what the Sea of Galilee looked like, the lake on whose banks Jesus met his first disciples and called them away from their fisherman's nets? Was not this the way in which the stories of the Bible took on form and structure? And did we not take the colors for these images from the world around us—just as the medieval artists when they portrayed the Bible stories did not invent the forms of human beings, cities, and landscapes, but took them from their own everyday world? But when we outgrow these images, when other pictures superimpose themselves upon our earlier images because in the meantime we have learned that Palestine lies far away, can we really dispense with a picture of the world which was the native home of the stories of the Bible?

What did the world of the Bible look like in reality? This is a question which everybody may have, whether he is familiar with the Bible or not. And indeed it is a question that might interest anybody. So it is my hope that your encounter with the pictures in this book will be accompanied by the expectation and the joy of a new discovery. It is of little importance whether your meeting turns out to be a corroboration or, what is more likely, a surprise or even a disappointment, compared with the pictures you have in your mind. For precisely when everything is different from what we imagined, these pictures can remind us that the stories of the Bible are not imaginary, but rather are part of a very real world.

I should like to make a second comment. The person who sets out for the Palestine of today is in search of the Palestine of yesterday. But the Palestine of yesterday does not simply show its face without search, for the Palestine of today has largely covered it up. Today Jerusalem is an Arabian city, and everywhere whole layers and strata of history seem to have overlaid the biblical past.

This may offend us, and presumably it does. But the perplexity we feel goes deeper than that. I suspect that even if we succeeded in removing all these strata, like archeologists who bit by bit dig down to the most ancient level of a city, we would still not have encountered the center of what constitutes the Bible. Archeological and historical research can help us to see more clearly the world in which the people of the Bible lived. This is no small thing, and for everybody who wants to understand the Bible it is a great boon. But that the event to which the Bible testifies reaches down to our own life, that God intervenes in the history of individual men and whole nations, that his Word lays hold of men and never lets them go again—this is quite a different matter. The authority of the Bible is a strange thing. It depends upon the world of the witnesses we hear in it. It depends upon the Lord of these witnesses, whom it may please to speak to us today through their words and thus turn what is far away into something very near, turn the past into the present. This archeology cannot do.

As I was preparing the pictures and the text of this book I was reliving the three months when I traveled between the Euphrates and the Nile. I took part in a tour sponsored by the German Protestant Institute for the Archeology of the Holy Land under the leadership of Professor D. Dr. Martin Noth. With his superior knowledge of the country and its history he brought Palestine very near to us. In addition to this I must express my gratitude to him for the kind interest he showed in the progress of this book and the pains he took in reading the text; every suggestion he made was helpful. But I must also express my thanks to my neighbor, Professor Dr. Rudolf Bohren, for many an exchange of views and frequent counsel.

All of the photographs were taken by the author with a Leica M 3 (Summicron 50 mm and Elmar 90 mm) on Agfa color reversal film. The numbers in the text (in parentheses) refer to the numbers of the pictures. A complete list of the pictures, which also serves as a table of contents, appears at the close of the book.

Since this book bears the title Landscapes of the Bible, one might think that it is concerned only with Palestine in the more restricted sense. And there are a number of illustrated books which deal primarily with the territory on both sides of the Jordan, between the Mediterranean Sea and the Syrian and Arabian Desert. In that case we should be exploring only a part of the small bridge of land between Egypt in the southwest and the Land of the Two Rivers (Mesopotamia) in the northeast. But would not our framework then be much too small? The horizon of the Bible itself extends farther. Beginning with its first pages, it ultimately encompasses the whole world. But, naturally, the world of the Bible was only the world

1 Bay of Beirut

9

as it was then known to its farthest borders, "to the ends of the earth." Israel's history took place within a very limited territory. Israel's vision, however, went far beyond these limits, as later the vision of primitive Christianity went beyond all limits. One need only think of the great prophets or the small book of the prophet Jonah—to say nothing of the Gospels and the letters of Paul, imbued as they are with the great commission which is directed to the whole world. Paul was convinced that he had been charged with a ministry that spanned the world; after all, it had fallen to him to establish the obedience of faith in the whole world to the honor of the name of his Lord (Rom. 1:5). His mission knew no limits. Therefore when he saw that his work was done in the east, it drove him on to Rome and the farthest reaches of the west. His final goal was Spain. The task before him was nothing less than traversing the world. The coasts of the Aegean Sea were especially familiar to him. His letters are either addressed to the young churches in this region or written from here, as was the letter to the Romans, which was to do quartermaster duty for him in Rome and contained his plan for Spain.

We can only suggest all this in a general way. The fact that the Bible has a world outlook is sometimes expressed in shorter or longer "tables of nations", which indicate the broad setting that is characteristic of the Bible. Thus in the very first book of the Bible we come upon a table of nations in which the world of that time was caught as it were in a net of astonishing breadth (Gen. 10). We ought not to think that we are so superior because our atlas covers the whole globe and no longer has any white patches in it (as the atlases still did a hundred years ago). We should rather be startled by the greatness of the horizon that opens up before us. Gerhard von Rad has written as follows on this point: "The broad range of vision is amazing for an inland people like Israel. It extends northward to the Black Sea, eastward to the Iranian plateau, southward to the coast of Somaliland, and westward to the Mediterranean coast of Spain. It is hard

to imagine that there was not an actual map corresponding to this literary

scheme." (Von Rad refers to Anaximander's map of the world as an

approximately contemporaneous example.) "In any case, considerable

work preceded it, and we may assume that Israel did only part of it and

made use of the knowledge of other nations (the Phoenicians)."

2 Nahr el-Kelb with Bridge   When the roll of the great profusion of peoples is called in this ancient

table of nations, the "hidden emotion that lies behind this dry enumeration is amazement and reverence at the riches of God's majestic creativity." In the language of the Psalms, "The earth is the Lord's and the fulness thereof, the world and those who dwell therein" (Ps. 24:1). So what we have here is not only geography! Rather, "the whole complex reality" in which the history of Israel took place is here "represented as God's creation." So even this prosaic survey of the world in a bare list of nations contains the faith of Israel—no high-sounding words about Israel's superiority over all the world (the name of Israel does not even appear in the list!), but manifestly a conviction that it has a Lord to whom the world belongs, that it sees the hand of this Lord everywhere, and that its existence is interwoven in the history of the world of nations. And what Israel learns and experiences at the hands of its God "is to occur exclusively in the realm of history." "Israel looked at herself in the midst of the interna-

3 Bas-relief at Nahr el-Kelb

12

tional world without illusion and quite unmythically" (Gerhard von Rad).
This book adopts the perspective within which Israel's history was enacted.
Hermann Gunkel once attempted to tell in the form of a parable the story
of Israel's rise in the context of the history of the great powers of the ancient
Orient: "A workshop. The day is Sunday. The laborers are resting and
the machines stand still. A small bird flies through an open window and

4 Porphyry Head of Rameses II

13

builds its nest beneath the great drop hammer. On Monday the machinery begins to move again; the hammer falls and smashes the nest. So during a lull in world-history, when the mighty antagonists of the Nile and Mesopotamia were at peace, the tribes of the children of Israel pushed their way into Palestine without knowing what they were doing. And when the great engine of history began to turn again they were crushed."

This is a striking simile. Obviously it oversimplifies the picture of Israel's history and cannot even suggest the many-stranded fabric of political relationships and tensions of which that history was a part. But it does express the involvement. And it is to that involvement that this book would point as it crosses the boundaries of Palestine proper and from the very outset begins with landscapes of the ancient Phoenician coasts from Tyre to Ugarit (including Sidon, Beirut, Byblos, and Amrit). And not content with this, at its close this book further attempts to illustrate the world perspective of the Bible by pushing beyond Damascus through the Syrian Desert to the Euphrates, which the Bible calls "the River" and which the Egyptians said "flowed backwards" because they judged everything by the Nile. Here we follow the course of the ancient caravan route through the oasis of Palmyra, which the Arabs call the "Bride of the Desert." When the Old Testament speaks of the patriarchs and the country of their origin, our sight is directed beyond the Euphrates. Abraham set forth at God's call from Haran (which the Akkadians called "Harranu" and which is situated east of the upper Euphrates). "Your fathers lived of old beyond the Euphrates . . ." (Josh. 24:2). In a text that contains a brief, succinct, almost creedal summary of the history of salvation, Jacob is called a "wandering Aramean" (Deut. 26:5) and thus is described as a nomad who drove his flocks back and forth between the desert and the cultivated lands. But it was also from beyond the Euphrates that the mighty empires of the Assyrians and the Babylonians invaded the history of Israel.

14

Finally, Egypt too cannot be omitted, for, after all, the shadow of the might of Egypt fell upon the very beginnings of Israel. This was the memory that Israel preserved throughout its whole history: "We were Pharaoh's slaves in Egypt" (Deut. 6:21). The historians have discovered in an ancient papyrus the report to his superior by an Egyptian frontier official from the eastern edge of the Nile delta. The report gives an account of the transit

5 Lion Plaque from Beth-Shean

15

of Bedouin tribes who were attempting to cross the border into Egypt with their flocks in order to "preserve their life" (Papyrus Anastasi VI from the period of the Pharaoh Seti II, circa 1215 B.C.).   So what Israel remembered from the early days of its history can be seen in the light of similar incidents that were ordinary happenings at that time.   We can also illustrate the conditions of forced labor under the Pharaohs by means of texts and wall paintings which describe related situations.   Slave laborers (by the thousands) were available in the Land of the Pharaohs.   Israel could never cease to remember its deliverance from the house of bondage which was Egypt, its liberation by the strong hand of God.

■

The landscapes in this book are capable of speaking for themselves. In the graphic speech of line and color they can bring very close to us the areas which we know from the pages of the Bible. It can be said of the

6 Byblos:
View from the Crusaders' Fortress

16

landscapes, though of course not of other features, that their general appearance has remained largely the same for thousands of years. Even Palestine's present lack of forest goes back to clearings of woodland in very early times. Arable land needed to be secured and the need for wood had to be supplied. Also largely unchanged are the simple processes of life: sowing, plowing, harvesting, threshing, winnowing, as well as the everyday life of the shepherd who moves across the country with his flock, but also the primitive forms of manual labor. Adolf Deissmann, the biblical scholar, was reminded of the ancient crafts and trades by the souks (markets) of present-day Oriental cities.

As a rule only small remainders of the ancient villages and towns are left, and for the most part they must still be wrested from the past by the slow and painstaking labor of the archeologists. The refined methods of excavation in use today have been described as "watchmaker's work" (Sir

7 Papyrus Reeds

Mortimer Wheeler). In many cases the ancient settlements still sleep unexplored beneath the rubble that covers them, even though we live in a time in which countless archeological discoveries of great importance have been made. Traveling in Palestine one frequently comes upon mounds with a characteristic form and color (cf., e.g., 26, 49). These are the rubbish heaps of ancient settlements which the Arabs call a tell. Tabular in form and gray in color, they stand out clearly from the surrounding country. Within them are a number of layers left by succeeding settlements, one above the other, since ordinarily after the destruction of a settlement the same site was used again; after all, it had been chosen in the first place because it provided the necessary conditions of life, such as a regular supply of water (cf. 32). The ground plan of the ancient towns is by our standards amazingly small. The towns were built to provide defense and therefore had to be extremely sparing of residential space within the city walls. We may speak of them as being fortresses of refuge. The Bronze Age and Early Iron Age Shechem, for example, was only about 750 feet long and 490 feet wide. This was the situation until the Hellenistic age, when the ground plans grew larger and the city planners were able to lay out grander designs. Archeology is a science (and a technique) by itself and involves the expert interpretation and dating of the various levels. And as is well known, it is here that the potsherds perform an indispensable service (68); for the shapes and decorations of the pottery make it possible to arrive at fairly precise conclusions with regard to their origin and age. The text which accompanies the landscapes in this book contents itself with providing a few aids toward seeing and understanding the pictures, occasionally indicating their geographical context, and here and there recalling the events which took place in these surroundings. Here at every step he who is familiar with the Bible will be flooded with recollections. Whether he walks through the narrow streets of the "ancient city" of Jerusalem or follows the track of the old Jericho Road "from Jerusalem to

8 Small Caravan of Amrit

18

Jericho" or wanders along the edge of the Plain of Jezreel, the stories of
the Bible attached to the landscape will leap to his mind.

∎

The title of this book is therefore intended to read as it does. We present
landscapes of the Bible and not an illustrated history of Israel, however
deeply landscape and history interpenetrate each other and however
saturated with history is the ground we tread.   These are not the impres-
sions recorded in a travel diary, though we have not wished to eliminate
all traces of our own experience.   Thus throughout the book it is the pictures which are our guide.   They are arranged in broad geographical
sequences.   We could not undertake to achieve completeness either in
the pictures or in the text.

9   Ancient Sanctuary at Amrit

ANCIENT PHOENICIAN
COASTS AND LEBANON

10 Spindle from Amrit (Royal Tomb)

Our first sequence of pictures begins with a view of the broad Bay of Beirut (1) and extends northward to Jebel el-Aqra on the Turkish border and southward to Tyre. In ancient times the Mediterranean shores of the present-day Arabian states of Lebanon and Syria were inhabited by the "ship-renowned" Phoenicians, as Homer calls them (Od., XV, 415). The Phoenicians were able to take advantage of the many natural harbors

as bases for their trading voyages, and throughout the Mediterranean region they established trading posts, factories, and counting houses. Sailing their ships of Tarshish (I Kings 10:22, Jonah 7:3), they advanced as far as Spain and among other exploits re-established Carthage as a Tyrian colony in the ninth century before Christ. In Phoenician Carthage means "new city." From the tenth century on, Tyre surpassed the hitherto more important Sidon. One can gain a vivid impression of the world-wide trade, the power, and the splendor of the island fortress of Tyre by reading Ezekiel 26–28. I wish that I could reprint these chapters here. In Chapter 27 the island city of Tyre is compared to a sumptuous ship built of the choicest materials. A cedar from Lebanon provides the mast, and the oars are fashioned from the oaks of Bashan (East Jordan). Her deck is made of pines from the coast of Cyprus, inlaid with ivory. (Ivory carving was one of the special feats of Phoenician craftsmanship.) The sail is made

11 Ugarit: View to the Sea

of fine embroidered linen from Egypt and her awning is blue and purple from the coasts of Elishah (to be equated with Cyprus). A proud list of suppliers: the best was none too good. Sidon and Arvad furnished the rowers, Zemer the pilots, and Byblos the caulkers. The whole coast was levied upon to provide an elite crew. Every detail of the picture obviously manifests an intimate knowledge of Tyre.

The importance of this ancient seafarer's coast is also reflected in the fact that the Egyptians adopted the technical terms of Canaanite navigation, whereas their own navigation was limited. For the most part they plied the coastline between the delta of the Nile and Byblos. The term "Byblos-transport" became a designation of a particular type of large ships which delivered papyrus (the writing material of antiquity from which comes our word "paper") and took on board in exchange the coveted cedar wood from Lebanon. Under Solomon we hear of Israel's taking

12 Ugarit: Excavations

23

part in maritime trade. This of course required relations with King Hiram of Tyre, who furnished Solomon's trading fleet with expert Phoenician seamen; it was also Hiram who supplied him with cedar wood and artisans for his building projects (I Kings 5:15ff.; 9:10ff.; 9:26f.; 10, 11, 22).

Added to the sea lanes were the overland routes, rounding out the picture of the far-flung network of international trade which existed even in early times. The land bridge of Syria-Palestine must be regarded as the most important traffic link known to the ancient East. Transportation-wise it lay at the center of the ancient world. Across this land bridge ran the traffic between Egypt on the one hand and Asia Minor and Mesopotamia on the other, not counting the tributaries, and the transit and import trade must have been very considerable.

■

We return, then, to Beirut (1). The wide-ranging bay is bordered by the Lebanon heights, which rise quickly to over nine thousand feet. When one flies from the international airport in Beirut to Damascus, the plane must first fly far out over the sea in order gradually to gain the altitude necessary to fly over Lebanon (and Anti-Lebanon). The name Lebanon means "white" (mountain); for a long time during the year it is covered (like Mount Hermon) with snow. The tourist literature of the state of Lebanon features the attraction that in certain months one can ski on the slopes of Lebanon and afterwards swim in the tropically warm sea—all on the same day.

The view of the Bay of Beirut shows a promontory which juts out into the sea near the center of the picture and stands out against its surroundings because of its somewhat lighter color. This is the cape at the mouth of the Nahr el-Kelb. The Nahr el-Kelb itself can be seen spanned by a medieval bridge not far from its mouth on another photograph. A part of the promontory fills the left margin of the picture (2). Today the road to Byblos

runs directly along the shore of the sea, whereas earlier it had to cross the promontory. Still discernible is the track of the ancient road on which the traders' caravans and the armies of the great powers wended their way long ago. Impressive witnesses of that past are the reliefs carved in the rock here, one of which, a double relief (3), is included in our series. These reliefs have been appropriately referred to as the "calling cards of world history." On the right-hand relief we encounter a typical scene which reminds us of the reliefs on the walls of Egyptian temples. As a matter of fact, it is an Egyptian representation. Egypt had laid its hand upon Syria and Palestine when its power permitted. Thus our scene illustrates the drama of world history. What we see is the Pharaoh sacrificing a prisoner

13   Forest North of Ugarit

to his god Amen-Re. The longer hieroglyphic inscription, however, is completely obscured by weathering except for the date: "in the year four." There is no doubt, however, that it is Rameses II (1304–1238) who followed the track of his great predecessor Thutmose III on this age-old highway of nations. Thutmose had undertaken no less than seventeen such campaigns and in 1480 had fought the famous battle of Megiddo on the Plain of Jezreel (27—28). In the fifth year of his reign Rameses II ventured battle with the Hittites of Asia Minor at Kadesh on the Orontes. Our no longer decipherable inscription is probably a triumphal account of a war like the many other texts we have concerning the battle at Kadesh. Incidentally, as we know, this battle was a very doubtful success; for according to the Hittite version Rameses was badly beaten, though he was spared a complete catastrophe. This defeat did not prevent the official Egyptian war report from ascribing to the Pharaoh a glorious victory, which it attributed to his own personal heroism, in accord with the style of the Egyptian war annals, since the god-king Pharaoh had to be invincible. Rameses himself zealously saw to it that the legend of victory was circulated abroad by means of inscriptions. Later there came a pact of mutual non-aggression between Egypt and the Hittite empire, which we have in duplicate texts (in hieroglyphs and cuneiform writing), and still later a political marriage between Rameses and a Hittite princess (circa 1267). Both great powers came to terms on the basis of a political balance of power.

We know the portrait of this undeniably great ruler, who was later known as the great conqueror and empire builder, from many representations. The Rameses figures on the façade of the rock-hewn temple at Abu Simbel are no less than sixty-five feet tall; Rameses loved colossal structures. We insert here the porphyry head which is now in the court of the mortuary temple of Rameses II at Luxor and shows the typical features of the Rameses portrait (4).

Between the right and the left relief (3) lies a span of centuries and during

that time the weight of political power shifted significantly. An Assyrian, immediately distinguishable by his beard, had his own figure carved into the rock close to that of the great Rameses. This was Shalmaneser III. He appeared upon the scene for the first time in 853, conquering the mighty Damascus, where he was faced by a coalition of "twelve princes," among them "Achabbu of Sir'al." This is the King Ahab of Israel (870–852) whom we know especially from the Elijah stories (I Kings 16:29 ff.). The battle took place at Karkar on the Orontes (26). Again, if we rely upon Shalmaneser's account, his enemies were destroyed. The modern historian, however, draws a different conclusion: "Since [Shalmaneser] did not pursue the conquered, he there at least suffered a reverse" (Wolfram von Soden). Also to the time of Shalmaneser III belongs the so-called Black Obelisk from Calah, which shows King Jehu kneeling before the tall figure of Shalmaneser, bringing tribute to him. The accompanying text

14   Jebel el-Aqra on the Turkish Border

calls him "Jehu of the house of Omri," which is not historically correct, since Jehu instead overthrew the dynasty of Omri (II Kings 9). Obviously, the Assyrians were not familiar with the exact circumstances.

Our relief on Nahr el-Kelb originated in connection with a later campaign of Shalmaneser against Damascus (841). It announces the Assyrians' claim to power over the land bridge of Syria-Palestine and thus already heralds the great political turning point the consequences of which would be increasingly felt by Israel too. In the years 722–721 Samaria fell into the hands of the Assyrians. The upper classes suffered the harsh fate of deportation, and Samaria became a province of the Assyrian Empire. Both measures were typical of the ruthless style of Assyrian rule. In 701 the troops of Sennacherib were at the gates of Jerusalem. We may assume that these events are familiar (cf. II Kings 17–19).

■

Even these meager references are sufficient to indicate the involvement of Israel's history in the turning wheels of history. The stone reliefs also tell a forceful tale precisely here, where two eras are, as it were, placed side by side. Rameses II belongs, of course, to the time before the tribes of Israel settled in Palestine; but he may have been the "Pharaoh of oppression" in whose reign the tribes of Israel were in slavery in Egypt. And thus his image brings us very close to the events reported in the Bible. But as we have seen, Shalmaneser III, also, cannot be separated from Israel's history any more than the later Assyrian kings under whose power Israel suffered can be excluded. From its very beginnings Israel was confronted by the politics of the great empires.

The prophets were alert to the course of political events. They saw at work in it the hand of God—and for them the masters of the world were God's instruments. They could not let the imperial style of the great powers go unchallenged, for they saw in it the boundless pride of man

reaching out to seize the whole earth. Thus one of the themes in the prophecy of Isaiah is the hubris of the Assyrian king, who, though he is commissioned by God, nevertheless goes beyond all bounds in his arrogance and thus forfeits his right. Isaiah portrays the Assyrian king uttering an imperial monologue that tells the whole story:

> "By the strength of my hand I have done it,
>> and by my wisdom, for I have understanding;
> I have removed the boundaries of peoples,
>> and have plundered their treasures; . . .
> My hand has found like a nest the wealth of the peoples;
>> and as men gather eggs that have been forsaken
>> so I have gathered all the earth;
> and there was none that moved a wing,
>> or opened the mouth, or chirped." (Isa. 10:13 ff.)

15 Harbor of Sidon

This sounds like an echo of the Assyrian annals of war. But it is in this very "style" that the Assyrian king oversteps the historical mandate assigned to him by God. Therefore Isaiah pronounces the judgment of God upon such hubris. The instrument of God sets himself up as the ruler of the world and thus comes into conflict with the true Lord of the world: "Shall the axe vaunt itself over him who hews with it, or the saw magnify itself against him who wields it?" (Isa. 10:15). Incidentally, one can compare this monologue of the Assyrian with Egyptian texts which read like parallels (Hugo Gressmann, Altorientalische Texte, 1926[2], pp. 18 ff.). And this instance does not exhaust the parallels. I think we may say that the Bible was not doing an injustice to the lords of the world when it attacked their style, when the prophets proclaimed the sole lordship of God over against the claims of the mighty. In the face of their grasping of the whole earth, the prophets could not do otherwise than remind men of the Lord of the earth, who holds even them in his sovereign hand. The prophets restored true proportion in a world that was losing all sense of proportion. So again we see that Israel was keeping in view the events of the world and was not merely occupied with itself. World history as a whole opens up before its eyes and is not merely a succession of unconnected individual incidents. In the rise and passing of the world empires—indeed, of all the nations in history—God shows that he is the Lord. Thus in Amos (9:7) God addresses this question to Israel: "Are you not like the Ethiopians to me, O people of Israel? ... Did I not bring up Israel from the land of Egypt, and the Philistines from Caphtor and the Syrians from Kir?" This outlook is characteristic of the prophets. Here history is not something that is subject to human interpretation; history and its concrete events are delivered into the hands of the Lord of the world. But the Lord of the world is none other than the God of Israel.

■

16 Tyre: North Harbor

Before we turn to Byblos, let me add one more small comment. A basalt relief showing in two panels, one above the other, a battle of lions and dogs (5) gives evidence of the high level which the art of representation had reached in the period around 1200 B.C. (the dating is Watzinger's). Although it was found in Beth-shean (fourteen miles south of the south end of the Sea of Galilee), its provenance must nevertheless be sought elsewhere—in North Syria? Galling would interpret it as a scene from a North Syrian zoological garden and therefore prefers to speak of lions and dogs as "playing". Or is Noth right in supposing that these are lions and lionesses playing? Zoological gardens were well known among Assyrian as well as Egyptian rulers, and a liking for exotic animals was widespread. Solomon too introduced apes and peacocks for the amusement of the royal court (I Kings 10:22). And hunting scenes appear again and again, as in the embossed work on the masterly golden bowl (1400–1300 B.C.) discovered in Ugarit on which a hunting scene runs round the rim, and a frieze of antelopes around the middle of the bowl further emphasizes the lively movement. Here form and content have found exemplary artistic representation.

■

What a contrast! While Beirut today is the most important port on the coast and a modern metropolis (with over 500,000 inhabitants), the once famous harbor of Byblos is covered with silt and Byblos itself is a small Arabian village. A distinguishing mark of Byblos visible from a great distance is a crusader's fortress, the tower of which reminds one of the belfries of medieval German castles. The crusaders, when they were in the Holy Land (between 1100 and 1300), built castles everywhere, often on the most precipitous mountain sites. We climbed up into the tower and looked out of a window over the ruins to the sea. In the foreground we could see the relatively young city of Byblos. The slender columns are the

remains of a Roman temple (6). The beginnings of ancient Byblos, however, go back to the late Stone Age. And as early as the end of the fourth millennium its relations with Egypt were established. Egyptian merchants stopped in Byblos and brought with them their gods. Foreign trade would have been a royal monopoly; the merchants bought and sold for the Pharaoh. Many archeological findings provide evidence of the intensive trading, in which cedar wood from Lebanon stood at the head of the list of imports for Egypt. A travel account of the Egyptian Wen-Amen, written around 1100 B.C., furnishes an extensive catalogue of goods given in exchange for cedar for the bark of Amen-Re, including five hundred rolls of papyrus besides gold and silver pitchers, fine linen, cowhides, rope, and bags. In consequence of centuries of exploitation Lebanon today is barren, and the proverbial "cedar from Lebanon" has become a rare article (19). The papyrus was extracted by a laborious process from the

17 Tyre: View to the South

33

pith of the stock of the papyrus plant and was furnished in various grades
(7). The Greeks, who secured the "paper" from Byblos, gave it the name
of this port of transshipment, and thus biblion became the word for "book,"
which also explains our word for the Book of books, "Bible." The oldest
manuscripts of the New Testament are papyrus texts, and we would think
of the letters of Paul as being originally written on papyrus. The durabi-

lity of the papyri was limited, but thousands of texts of varying contents, discovered mainly in the dry sands of Egypt, still provide us today with valuable glimpses into the everyday life of people around the time of the New Testament. Marriage contracts, commercial contracts, accounts, letters, and so on—everything was recorded on papyrus, in skilled or awkward handwriting. A bygone world comes alive again for us. And

19 Cedars on Jebel el-Baruk

35

this is important for the understanding of the New Testament, as Deiss-mann was one of the first to show.

■

On the road to Ugarit lies Amrit, within sight of the ancient Phoenician island of Arvad. A small "caravan" approaches us, consisting of a donkey, the riding animal, and a camel carrying the load. Behind them, barely discernible in the distance, emerges from the sea the island of Arvad, which today is no more than a fishing village (8). We get an impression of Amrit's past from the Phoenician sanctuary, which originally must have stood in the midst of a pool, as the high basement and circular border around the whole structure would indicate. The image of the god was located in the shrine above, which is ornamented with Egyptian fluting (9). A grave monument with lion heads (indicating royal insignia), here preserved with other burial structures, belongs to a later—Hellenistic—period (10). The Arabs call these royal graves the "spindles of Amrit."

■

Ancient Ugarit lies directly opposite the eastern point of Cyprus on the Ras esh-Shamra, the "fennel head" (in the same way the Greek word Marathon means "fennel field"). Even today fennel grows among the excavated remains of the royal city dating from the middle of the second century. These remains have been excavated by the French in a series of campaigns since 1929 under the leadership of Claude Schaeffer. An accidental find led to the discovery of the ancient settlement. From the green trees on the edge of the excavation field our gaze runs past the coastal strip to the "white harbor" (Minet el-Beda) and the sea (11). What a treasure was brought to light here! The palace has its great inner court, and its fountain, from which we drank water as delectable as in the days of the kings of Ugarit. The city is of considerable dimensions (the palace alone covers

9,700 square feet), with a street of shops, comparable to the souks of present-day Oriental cities, and temples, whose foundations have been exposed. But most important of all are the great "libraries," containing undreamed-of treasures, important for the light they throw not only upon historical relations and cultural links but also upon religious ideas; for among the finds were mythological texts, rituals for festival worship, etc.

Here a whole world is opened up, the world of a highly developed and widely ramified culture, such as the Israelite tribes found when they arrived in Palestine. Among the literary texts are many word lists (glossaries), which show how the language areas overlapped because of world-wide contacts and how the effort was made to understand the language of others. One of the vocabularies is actually quadrilingual; the same word

21 Urginea maritima

appears in Sumerian, Akkadian, Hurrian, and Ugaritic. The Ugaritic language is related to the Phoenician. Unfortunately, we cannot go into the details of the language or the related subject of the script in which it was written. The hitherto unknown cuneiform alphabet of Ugarit of thirty characters was quickly deciphered. Incidentally, the Phoenicians transmitted the alphabetic script to the Greeks, who adopted it around 900 B.C.

The expositor of the Bible is especially enriched by the mythological texts discovered in Ugarit, for they give him an insight into the Ugaritic religion. In mythological form he finds here an interpretation of the processes of life and death in the dying and revival of the god Baal, who is first killed by Mot, the god of death, when Anat intervenes, kills Mot, and raises Baal to life again. This is a segment of the world of cultic myths with which Israel was surrounded. Here we feel a breath of it and we understand

22 Source of the Litani
with View of Anti-Lebanon

39

why this world confronted Israel with a striking alternative to its own faith which forced it to say a clear Yes or No. Comparable to these finds in importance are, for example, the newly discovered Gnostic texts from Nag-Hamadi in Upper Egypt, which throw more light upon Gnosticism, the great movement with which the early church had to struggle, as even the letters of Paul show. The people of the Bible did not live on a religious island; they were compelled to preserve and testify to their faith in a world that was very near, but very alien, to them.

We mentioned above the considerable dimensions of ancient Ugarit. This size must not, however, be confused with spaciousness. The space within the ancient cities was actually quite small, as is apparent from our picture of part of the excavations (12). The city gate of Ugarit was a small opening in the wall, which is understandable considering that the ancient cities were fortresses. Suffering invasion from the so-called Peoples of the Sea, the city must have been destroyed around 1200 B.C. The Philistines, so frequently mentioned in the Old Testament, belonged to these Peoples of the Sea (cf. 98).

Looking northward from Ugarit in clear weather we can make out against the rim of the horizon the mountain of the gods of Ugarit mentioned in the cuneiform texts. This is Jebel el-Aqra. The Arabian name characterizes it immediately. It is a "baldpate" in the midst of wooded country (14). For it was a great surprise, which perhaps can be fully appreciated only by one who has traveled in the lands of the Bible, that on the journey to what was to be for us the northernmost point on the coast we should be surrounded by a tall forest of Aleppo pines. One of the photographs taken on the way, opposite Ras el-Bassit (13) exhibits the charm of this forest landscape. The sea stands out only in pale relief, dissolving in the haze.

■

Of the coastal cities of Phoenicia in ancient times we still have not discussed Tyre and Sidon. They also appear in the New Testament, and in

this order, which goes back to Palestine itself. In the Gospels we are told

that Jesus stopped as he was passing through the neighborhood of Tyre

and Sidon and healed the daughter of a Syrophoenician woman (Mark

7:24–30). We should also realize that at that time the territory of Tyre ex-

tended to the border of northern Galilee. In Matthew the woman is spoken

of in more old-fashioned terms as a "Canaanite woman," and this evan-

23   Ba'albek:
      Columns of the Temple of Jupiter

41

gelist quite obviously understands the story as a symbolic anticipation of the calling of all nations (Matt. 15:21–28).

Coming from Beirut we reach Sidon first. A photograph of the harbor taken in the evening catches the iridescence of the setting sun upon the water (15). Toward evening the contours become especially clear. The warm tone of the late light imparts a glow to the whole scene and also touches the silhouette of the crusader's castle which dominates the entrance to the harbor.

Ancient Tyre is situated farther south (16—17). The glory of this island citadel was destroyed with the coming of Alexander the Great. In the year 332 B.C., when Alexander, pursuing his grand strategy, came down the coast on his way to Egypt in order to cover his rear before pushing on to the east, Arvad, Byblos, and Sidon had already capitulated. Tyre offered resistance after the initial negotiations broke down. Alexander

24 Lebanon from Ba'albek

42

constructed a mole two thousand feet long and two hundred feet wide from the mainland to the island and over it brought up mobile siege machinery higher than had ever been built before. Twenty stories high, it towered above the city wall. But even after all these preparations, carried out with all the available means of military technology, the city was not reduced until seven months later with the aid of a fleet of two hundred ships which Alexander, hitherto "so averse to the sea" (Ernst Kornemann), brought down from Sidon. Alexander's mole is still discernible today, widened on both sides by shifting sand.

One can walk around ancient Tyre in about an hour. Then one's eyes can follow the curve of the coast across the Ladder of Tyre to the south (17), where just beyond the limits of sight lies the territory of the present-day state of Israel. Meanwhile we have come about fourteen miles (as the crow flies) closer to it.

25 Tributary of the Orontes
     Near Lebwe

43

We leave the coast now and ascend southward from Beirut to Lebanon, searching for the cedars on Jebel el-Baruk. Long before we have reached them we see them standing in lonely height (5,700 feet). Along with the stand of cedars at Bsherri, which as a tourist attraction is better known, these trees constitute the small remainder of the former abundance of forest, not counting the occasional cedars one sees here and there. A view from the ascent shows the barren slope of Lebanon to the sea, though the impression received from the landscape remains extraordinarily colorful (18). Looking at the cedars, one feels that all the printed descriptions are inadequate, so majestically do they stand on the slopes, with mighty trunks, bold, impressive outlines, and symmetrical branches (19). We see why the state of Lebanon has a cedar on its coat of arms.

Directly alongside the cedars grow the thistles, which are met with throughout the country (20). The reader of the Bible is reminded of Adam's ground bringing forth thorns and thistles; for the Bible does not hide the hard side of life, the hard labor and the meager return. It expresses all this with a dry realism in the much too little read book of Ecclesiastes: "I considered all that my hands had done and the toil I had spent in doing it, and behold, all was vanity and a striving after wind . . ." (Eccles. 2:11).

Looking at the next picture (21) one would like to think of the lilies of the field and Jesus' words in the Sermon on the Mount, that even Solomon in all his glory was not arrayed like one of these. Botanically, however, these are probably (according to Gustaf Dalman) Urginea maritima, which we saw frequently despite the rainless months (cf. 40, 64). They thrive even in the Desert of Judah and are offered for sale by Bedouin boys in the streets of Jerusalem.

If one climbs some 650 feet above the cedars on Jebel el-Baruk one can look out from the summit upon the broad plain between Lebanon and Anti-Lebanon. It bears the name of Beka and is crossed by the Litani in the south and the Orontes in the north.

Both rivers rise not too far from each other. This plain, which was formerly much more thickly populated, is geologically speaking a rift valley that extends southward into the Jordan rift, going beyond the Dead Sea into the Wadi el-Araba and the Gulf of Aqaba. At the Dead Sea we find ourselves at the lowest spot on the whole surface of the earth. Its surface level is 1,300 feet below that of the Mediterranean, while the Dead Sea itself at its deepest point has a depth of 1,300 feet. These geological and geographical facts explain, among other things, the peculiar climatic conditions of the Jordan valley — its tropical temperature of from 95 to 120 degrees Fahrenheit. The road "from Jerusalem to Jericho" has a gradient of 3,280 feet in 23 miles, since the old city of Jerusalem lies on an average of 2,400 feet above and Jericho 820 feet below the sea level.

We show the source of the Litani with Anti-Lebanon in the background

26 Karkar near the Nosairian Range

(22). Nearby is the site of the great Roman temple of Ba'albek, a mighty complex of buildings dating back to the second century after Christ. Only six of the original fifty-four columns of the temple of Jupiter still remain (23), but even these have an imposing effect. If you will look very closely, you will see some tourists in the lower left corner of the picture. They may provide a scale for the size of the columns, which tower up sixty-five feet. A broad terraced staircase leads up to the temple. Everything is on a large scale, impressing upon us the might of the Imperium Romanum. From Ba'albek we look across once more to Lebanon, whose ridges still (in late August!) show a few very small patches of snow which the sun has almost melted away (24). Bearing north we cross a tributary of the Orontes (25). The last picture in this first sequence (26) reminds us of the beginning. We find ourselves in the broad plain of the Orontes at Kar-kar, midway between Aleppo and Ugarit, and when we mentioned the

27 Plain of Jezreel

reliefs at Nahr el-Kelb (3) we were already speaking about Karkar. The two unmistakable mounds of the city rise from the plain before the range of the Nosairian Mountains, a site which has not yet been exploited archeologically. It was here in the year 853 B.C. that the mighty army of the Assyrian Shalmaneser III clashed with the coalition of Palestinian-Syrian kings. No less than three Assyrian accounts have been found, all of them triumphal paeans for Shalmaneser. The number of losses which Shalmaneser inflicted upon his opponents varies from account to account, ranging from 14,000 to 25,000. It is evident that the modern historian must add a question mark to such reports of victorious armies. Shalmaneser crossed the Euphrates "during its flood," which is emphasized in all the texts as an unusual feat, and came by way of Aleppo. Even before he reached the Orontes his march was one victory after another. We have already noted that Ahab of Israel took part in the coalition against Shal-

28   Plain of Jezreel (close-up)

47

maneser (with 2,000 chariots and 10,000 men). According to one of the accounts Karkar went up in flames.

Today the plain presents a very peaceful picture. Flocks of sheep pass us by. They come from the nearby watering place, located in the small village of Karkur. The village has inherited the ancient name, only slightly altered in modern Arabic, as is often the case. Where the battle raged long ago, broad cotton fields, which had just been harvested, stretch out across the plain, as they do also south of Damascus and along the Euphrates.

After this prelude we turn to Palestine in the narrower sense of the word. A look at the map reveals how small Palestine actually is. The distance between the towns of Dan and Beersheba, mentioned by the Old Testament itself as the approximate northern and southern boundaries, is not more than 150 miles. The south end of the Sea of Galilee is only a little over sixty miles from the north shore of the Dead Sea. If one were to travel in a straight line from Tiberias on the western shore of the Sea of Galilee to the eastern coast of the Mediterranean, the distance would be about thirty miles.

But perhaps the language of mere numbers is too pallid to convey the diminutiveness of the country. The small compass of Palestine becomes very real when one experiences it on the spot. Thus on a clear day one can stand on the heights of the West Jordanian mountains — say, on Mount Gerizim (near Shechem) — and easily see as far as the Mediterranean coast in the west and as far as the mountains on the other side of the Jordan in the east. The limited extent of the country can also be brought home by comparing the distances with those in our own homeland. The results cannot fail to be surprising.

The distances in our conception of Palestine, which are usually set too high, quickly dwindle to a fraction, so circumscribed is its area, so diverse are its forms of landscape. Mountain regions with deeply gouged valleys alternate with fertile plains. But there are also areas which are like the steppe and the desert. Moreover, only a relatively small number of inhabitants has ever been able to live on the yield of the soil, eating their bread "in the sweat of their face." If Palestine was called the land "flowing with milk and honey," those who so characterized it were thinking of the contrast between the cultivated land and the poverty of the desert.

■

In the first picture the broad Plain of Jezreel opens up before us (27). We are looking from the southern edge of the plain (not far from Jenin) to-

29 Nablus (Flavia Neapolis)
    Between Ebal and Gerizim

49

ward the mountains of Lower Galilee. The brown earth, which after the months of summer drought still shows some traces of green, indicates the great fertility of the soil. It is no accident that the (pre-Isrealite?) name Jezreel means "God sows." Near the right margin of the picture we recognize Mount Tabor by its perfectly rounded shape. A second view (28) brings a section of the landscape somewhat closer. Near the center of the picture, above a ravine running upwards from the plain, a suggestion of houses can be seen. These are the houses at the highest point of Nazareth. So close are we here to the village of Jesus' boyhood! The shapes of the Lower Galilean hill country are like those of the mountains of Samaria adjacent to the Plain of Jezreel on the south — not harsh but rather soft contours. If one were able to look farther to the west, he would see the famous Mount Carmel of the Elijah stories on the horizon.

Again landscape and history are closely linked. At the opening of the pass at Megiddo, Pharaoh Thutmose III, coming up from the south in 1480 B.C., met the troops of a great coalition under the leadership of the prince of Kadesh and won a brilliant victory. His opponents did not utilize their strategically favorable position and failed to block the pass. But there was another battle, "at Taanach, by the waters of Megiddo," after the invasion of the tribes of Israel had succeeded, in the time of Deborah, the prophetess. This time it was against Sisera. This strange, perhaps Illyrian, name has caused the scholars to surmise that he is to be associated with the so-called "Peoples of the Sea," who around 1200 B.C. were coming from the west by land and sea, invading the entire coastal region from Asia Minor to Egypt. Despite his dreaded chariots, Sisera lost the battle against the Israelite forces led by Barak. This great event is reflected in one of the oldest parts of the Old Testament, the song of Deborah (Judg. 5). The "chariots" were iron-clad vehicles drawn by horses (Judg. 4:3), which had been introduced by the Hyksos into the world of the ancient Orient. In the reign of Solomon we hear of chariot cities and cities

for horsemen, which were the military garrisons he built (I Kings 9:19; 10:26 ff.).

The song of Deborah gives us a vivid impression of the precarious position of the Israelite tribes and indicates the varying part the individual tribes played in the battle. But he who is really acting here is Israel's God, who takes up the cause of his people:

" Hear, O kings; give ear, O princes; to the Lord I will sing,

I will make melody to the Lord, the God of Israel.

Lord, when thou didst go forth from Seir,

when thou didst march from the region of Edom,

the earth trembled, and the heavens dropped,

yea, the clouds dropped water.

The mountains quaked before the Lord,

yon Sinai before the Lord, the God of Israel.

30 Shechem:
Excavations at North Gate

In the days of Shamgar, son of Anath,

    in the days of Jael, caravans ceased

    and travelers kept to the byways.

The peasantry ceased in Israel, they ceased

    until you arose, Deborah,

    arose as a mother in Israel.

31   Torah Scroll of the Samaritans

When new gods were chosen,

    then war was in the gates.

Was shield or spear to be seen

    among forty thousand in Israel?

My heart goes out to the commanders of Israel

    who offered themselves willingly among the people.

    Bless the Lord.

Tell of it, you who ride on tawny asses,

    you who sit on rich carpets

    and you who walk by the way.

To the sound of musicians at the watering places,

    there they repeat the triumphs of the Lord,

Torah Scroll of the Samaritans (31)

the triumphs of his peasantry in Israel.

Then down to the gates marched the people of the Lord.

Awake, awake, Deborah!

    Awake, awake, utter a song!

Arise, Barak, lead away your captives,

    O son of Abinoam.

Then down marched the remnant of the noble;

    the people of the Lord marched down for him against the mighty.

From Ephraim they set out thither into the valley,

    following you, Benjamin, with your kinsmen;

from Machir marched down the commanders,

    and from Zebulun those who bear the marshal's staff;

the princes of Issachar came with Deborah,

    and Issachar faithful to Barak;

    into the valley they rushed forth at his heels.

Among the clans of Reuben

    there were great searchings of heart.

Why did you tarry among the sheepfolds,

    to hear the piping for the flocks?

Among the clans of Reuben

    there were great searchings of heart.

Gilead stayed beyond the Jordan;

    and Dan, why did he abide with the ships?

Asher sat still at the coast of the sea,

    settling down by his landings.

Zebulun is a people that jeoparded their lives to the death;

    Naphtali too, on the heights of the field.

The kings came, they fought;

    then fought the kings of Canaan,

at Taanach, by the waters of Megiddo. . . ." (Judg. 5:3–19)

In the times of the Judges also falls the defeat that Gideon inflicted upon the Midianites at the southwest exit from the plain as they pressed in once again from the eastern desert, riding their swift camels without number (Judg. 6 ff.).

It was in the same valley of battles that Saul lost his kingdom and his life when he was obliged to place himself in a hopeless situation over against the Philistines. Saul, already wounded by an arrow, fell upon his own sword. Here his three sons also met death. And David lamented over Saul and Jonathan, to whom he was bound by close friendship:

"In life and in death they were not divided; they were swifter than eagles, they were stronger than lions . . . How are the mighty fallen in the midst of the battle!" (II Sam. 1:23, 25)

32   Well Scene at Tell el-Farah (Tirzah)

It was on this plain that Jehu, the officer whom Elisha had designated as king, seized the kingdom in a swift surprise attack. Immediately after the army had proclaimed him king, he raced with his chariot and a small escort to the city of Jezreel, where Ahaziah of Judah was visiting Joram of Israel, shot Joram with his own hand, and pursued the fleeing Ahaziah until he too was done to death (II Kings 9). The deed of Jehu is still remembered in the prophecy of Hosea. The Lord tells Hosea to name his first son Jezreel: "Call his name Jezreel; for yet a little while, and I will punish the house of Jehu for the blood of Jezreel, and I will put an end to the kingdom of the house of Israel. And on that day, I will break the bow of Israel in the valley of Jezreel" (Hos. 1:4–5). Barely a century and a half later, in the year 609, King Josiah went to meet Pharaoh Neco, who was on his way north. The account says with extreme concision that

33 Jebel Ferdesh.
    Bedouin Family in Foreground

56

Pharaoh "slew him at Megiddo, when he saw him" (II Kings 23). It would appear that not even a battle was needed to dispose of him.

■

In the middle of the Samaritan hill country, between Mount Gerizim and Mount Ebal, lies present-day Nablus (29). The name of this Arab settlement barely betrays its original form: Flavia Neapolis. This was its name when it was rebuilt in 72 A.D. in honor of the emperor Flavius Vespasian. Nablus is a later settlement of ancient Shechem, which is situated a mile and a half east of Nablus in the direction in which the picture looks. Shechem played an important role in the history of Israel. Here is where the northern and southern tribes joined together under Joshua. In Shechem, as later in Bethel and Shiloh and under David in Jerusalem, the sacred ark, the empty throne of the God of Israel, was kept.

34 Women Carrying Fuel

The site of Shechem was settled as early as 4000 B.C. Excavations have uncovered, among other things, the Bronze Age north gate of the city defenses, whose mighty proportions can only be described as imposing (30). The gate exhibits a well-planned system of two consecutive gate-chambers. From the front chamber it was possible to reach the top by steps on both sides. The outer and inner gates are each flanked and additionally secured by towers. The whole structure shows Babylonian influences. Our picture can only give a general impression.

■

In Nablus today only a small remnant of Samaritans reminds us of the Samaritans of the Bible. We know that after a long history of tensions and conflicts, they separated from the Temple cultus in Jerusalem, presumably at the beginning of the Hellenistic period, though it is not possible to fix a more exact date. As is well known, they appear frequently in the New Testament, — for example, in the story of Jesus' meeting with the Samaritan woman at Jacob's well (John 4), the story of the refusal to give hospitality in a Samaritan village (Luke 9:52 ff.), and the parable of the Good Samaritan (Luke 10:30–37). Always the antagonism between the Jews and the Samaritans can be felt, and in the days of Jesus this tension increased rather than relaxed. But Jesus himself took no part in the antagonism. On the contrary, he shows the Good Samaritan acting more exemplarily than the representatives of Israel, and he asks the Samaritan woman for a drink of fresh water. He did not accept the heritage of antagonism.

The Samaritans had established their own sanctuary on Mount Gerizim, as is shown by John 4. Thus the Samaritan woman says to Jesus at the well of Jacob, "'Our fathers worshiped on this mountain; and you say that in Jerusalem is the place where men ought to worship.' Jesus said to her, 'Woman, believe me, the hour is coming when neither on this moun-

35 Young Shepherds on Jebel Ferdesh

58

tain nor in Jerusalem will you worship the Father. You worship what you

do not know; we worship what we know, for salvation is from the Jews.

But the hour is coming, and now is, when the true worshipers will worship

the Father in spirit and truth, for such the Father seeks to worship him.

God is spirit, and those who worship him must worship in spirit and truth.'

The woman said to him, 'I know that Messiah is coming (he who is called   36 Jebel Ferdesh: Buildings of Herod

Christ); when he comes, he will show us all things.' Jesus said to her, 'I who speak to you am he' " (John 4:20–26).

The Samaritans still celebrate the Feast of the Passover according to their usage on Mount Gerizim. On separating from Jerusalem they took with them the five books of Moses as their holy scriptures. Their Torah scroll, photographed in the entrance of their synagogue in Nablus, is written in the Samaritan script (31).

Our photograph also prompts us to look into the development of the book. The scroll form, which the Bible presupposes when it speaks of the book, survived into the fourth century after Christ. I mention here only the moving scene contained in the book of Jeremiah.

In Jeremiah 36 we are told that Jeremiah dictated the words of his prophecy to his helper Baruch, who wrote them upon a scroll and then read them in the Temple in the hearing of all the people. King Jehoiakim

37   Jebel Ferdesh in Evening Light

61

heard of this incident and commanded that the scroll be brought to him. "And Jehudi read it to the king and all the princes who stood beside the king. It was the ninth month [December], and the king was sitting in the winter house and there was a fire burning in the brazier before him. As Jehudi read three or four columns, the king would cut them off with a penknife and throw them into the fire in the brazier, until the entire scroll was consumed in the fire that was in the brazier. Yet neither the king, nor any of his servants who heard all these words, was afraid, nor did they rend their garments. Even when Elnathan and Delaiah and Gemariah urged the king not to burn the scroll, he would not listen to them" (Jer. 36:21 b–25).

The present book form arose at the end of the first century after Christ and became increasingly common, the pages being laid in tiers upon each other.

In the course of their long history the Samaritans dwindled in numbers and became a "historical curiosity" (Martin Noth). Their number at present is given at about 250 and is divided between Nablus and Jaffa.

■

About seven miles northeast of Shechem lies Tell el-Farah. Roland de Vaux believes that it is the Tirzah of the Old Testament, which for a time was the residence of the Israelite kings until Omri established a new royal residence on the hill of Samaria (1 Kings 16:23–24). At the foot of Tell el-Farah we met women in picturesque, many-colored dresses, coming to draw water (32). With great skill they carry the waterpots on their heads as in ancient times — a typical picture which reminds us of biblical scenes associated with wells. In this arid country we understand why Jewish law prescribed that in the desert a pot of honey should be emptied if it were a question of saving the water in a damaged pot (Gustaf Dalman). For

here the elementary rule obtained: "Water keeps a man alive in the desert, not honey."

■

At the edge of the Desert of Judah rises Jebel Ferdesh (about three miles southeast of Bethlehem). Its flattened summit is noticeable (33), for this is the work of human hands. On this summit there was once a fortress of refuge, built by Herod the Great (37–4 B.C.), the remains of which can still be seen. Climbing the mountain, one sees a large, partially walled circle about 150 feet in diameter (36). In addition to the castle on the heights there were other buildings at the foot of the mountain.

38   View of the City of Hebron

Herod built or rebuilt a whole series of such fortresses, including, for example, the almost inaccessible Masad, the citadel of Cyprus above Jericho, the Alexandrium, and the fortress of Machaerus, which is familiar from the story of John the Baptist. We begin to see how preoccupied Herod was with his safety and that of his family. The structure on Jebel Ferdesh bore the name Herodium. When Herod died in Jericho in 4 B.C., it was here that he was buried with great ceremony, as we read in Josephus' account.

We must also mention here that Herod the Great was a great builder in other respects; one comes upon traces of him throughout the country. His political position (in the framework of the Roman Empire he was a so-called "confederate king") is reflected in his use of the names of the Caesars for the cities he established. Thus he changed the name of ancient Samaria to Sebaste (in Greek, the city of Augustus) and erected an imposing temple of Augustus on the commanding heights of the mountain, the outside staircase of which still exists today. He also created Caesarea with its harbor, Sebastos harbor, built at great expense over a period of twelve years, a very considerable feat of urban construction. The names of Caesars were also attached to buildings and cities established by the sons of Herod. Thus Tiberias on the Sea of Gennesaret goes back to Herod Antipas, the reigning sovereign in the time of Jesus (in honor of Tiberius!), as Caesarea Philippi was built by Herod's son Philip. Like Herod's Sebaste, this "imperial city" was built in honor of Augustus. We shall come back later to the building activity of Herod the Great in Hebron and Jerusalem. His zeal for construction extended even beyond the borders of his own land. He made himself useful also in Tyre, Sidon, Beirut, Byblos, Tripoli and Damascus, and even in Athens and Rhodes. Not only is all this important for the general picture of Herod the Great, who was in this respect following the style of the Diadochi, but it also opens up perspectives for understanding the political situation of Pale-

stine in the Herodian period. Herod's role as a great builder was possible only because he kept a tightly organized government, which with all its severity was not without a certain breadth of mind, and made a constant effort to secure the favor of the world power of that day, an effort which was always shrewdly accommodated to every political vicissitude. Herod succeeded in gaining the favor of Augustus, even though he had previously enjoyed the support of Antony. Existing as Herod did in the shadow of the power of world-embracing imperium, this policy of his also involved the problem of his relationship to the people he ruled. He was unable to gain their good will. Even the erection of the Temple in Jerusalem and the buildings in Hebron, by which he sought to indulge the Jewish tradition, though he himself had no sympathy with it, did not change this attitude. For the Jewish people he remained a foreigner and the cleft was unbridgeable, even apart from all the complicating details of his reign. Knowing

39   Hebron: Mosque with Minaret

65

these circumstances, one also grasps more concretely that scene in the Gospels in which the question of Caesar's right to collect the tax money appears (Mark 12:13–17 and parallels). The Pharisees and also the adherents of Herod (this Herod is Herod Antipas, the son of the great Herod, the sovereign Lord of Jesus) were naturally interested in this question, or rather Jesus' answer to it, since for them it affected the structure of the state. They were obviously expecting a negative answer. Jesus' reply acknowledges Ceasar's right, but limits it by the claim that God has upon man. But this limits Caesar himself and subjects him to the superior power of God — just as for the prophets too the lords of the world were in the hands of God. One might also think here of the Pilate scenes in the Gospel of John (John 18:28 ff.). The representative of Caesar thinks he can say to Jesus, "Do you not know that I have power to release you, and power to crucify you?" But Jesus' answer was "You would have no power over me unless it had been given you from above" (John 19:10–11).

A few words more about the pictures of Jebel Ferdesh. The first and the last views show it as light changes from morning to late afternoon (33—37). The Bedouin family in the foreground (33) were living in the tent which is visible on the left of the picture. On the way we met women laden with bundles of sticks for fuel (34). Young Bedouin shepherds in typical Bedouin clothes and homemade shoes accompanied us to the top of the mountain (35). From there we had a broad view all around, including the Dead Sea, Bethlehem, and the towers on the Mount of Olives in Jerusalem, and not far away Tekoa, the home of the prophet Amos.

■

On the way south (in the direction of Beersheba) we arrived at Hebron (38). Ancient Hebron probably was situated on the height from which our picture was taken (Jebel er-Rumede). We are familiar with Hebron from the stories of Abraham in the Bible. Here too David was anointed king of

the "house of Judah" until finally he was offered the kingship of the tribes of Israel and he united both states into one. In this new situation he shrewdly chose a new capital, Jerusalem, which he still had to conquer.

The modern Arabic name for Hebron is el-Khalil, "the friend." This is a reminder of Abraham's connection with Hebron, since among the Arabs "the friend" is a title of honor for Abraham, the friend of God (cf. Isa. 41:8; II Chron. 20:7; Jas. 2:23).

Our photograph presents the modern city of Hebron with its great Mosque of Abraham and its minaret. The history of this mosque, in which the graves of the patriarchs are exhibited, goes back to Herod the Great, who built here a "smaller copy of the Temple area in Jerusalem" (C. Watzinger).

40 South from Hebron: Sel ed-Dilbe

The outer wall is divided by pilasters which form the "footing" and are proportioned according to the Roman unit-measure. The difference in structure and color clearly shows the line between the Herodian and the later wall (39). About four miles south-west of Hebron is the "Valley of Plane Trees" (Sel ed-Dilbe), whose abundance of water is used today for the large plantations here (40). We may conjecture that the "springs" mentioned in Joshua 15:19 were located here (Martin Noth). The care that is taken of the trees is plain to be seen. A little farther south we catch a glimpse of the Negeb, the "Dry Land", shimmering in the harsh light of the noonday sun.

The Lake of Gennesaret! (41) This appears here in our sequence of pictures because we are looking at it from the southeast. We are at the juncture of three countries. The drums of fallen columns and remains of walls remind us of ancient Gadara (Matt. 8:28–34), whose earlier importance (it once had a university) can still be inferred from the remains of two small theaters. Only six miles separate us from the south end of the lake. Today the Jordanian town of Umm Kes is located here. In the foreground is the Yarmuk valley, beyond which Syrian territory begins and runs to the eastern shore of the lake. As our eye follows the blue surface of the lake it falls upon the Galilean highland which belongs to the state of Israel. Tiberias remains hidden in the mist.

The fishermen living on the shore called the lake "the Galilean Sea", whereas Luke, the Hellenist who had traveled in the Mediterranean world, called it a lake. On its northern shore were the cities that heard Jesus' message: "Repent, for the kingdom of heaven is at hand." We need only to

68

mention the familiar name of Capernaum to quicken our memory of the stories in the Gospels which took place here. On the shore of the lake Jesus called his first disciples, "and immediately they left their nets and followed him" (Mark 1:18). Becoming his disciples, they sailed with him across the lake and when the storm overtook them they woke him from sleep (Matt. 3:23–27). It was in Capernaum that the centurion entreated him, "Only say the word, and my servant will be healed." Accustomed to command, he credited Jesus with a power to command even where all human power fails (Matt. 8:5–13). But we cannot even mention all the stories.

It is not by chance that Capernaum is called "his" city, for "in all Palestine there was no place where the memories were so numerous as in Capernaum" (Gustaf Dalman). Apart from Jerusalem, no other city is so firmly anchored in the traditon. But a saying which is recorded in Matthew 11:20–24 (and Luke 10:13–16) mentions still other nearby cities as places

where Jesus worked: "Woe to you, Chorazin! woe to you, Bethsaida! for if the mighty works done in you had been done in Tyre and Sidon, they would have repented long ago in sackcloth and ashes. But I tell you, it shall be more tolerable on the day of judgment for Tyre and Sidon than for you". If here the memory of the tradition was lost, today the cities themselves, including Capernaum, belong to the past. They experienced the

42 Landscape Near Pella

same fate that befell so many cities of Old Testament times. Only meager remains have survived from which the archeologists deduce their former location. Tiberias is an exception; it still stands today. But whether Jesus ever visited Tiberias, the residence of his sovereign, we do not know.

Gadara belonged to Decapolis, the league of ten cities which is mentioned occasionally in the Gospels and which, excepting Scythopolis (the

43 Forest in the Ajlun

71

ancient Beth-Shean, included cities in the territory of East Jordan, such as Pella, Gerasa, and Philadelphia. They were directly subject to the Roman province of Syria and were permitted to govern themselves independently. As Hellenistic cities they contained only a minority of Jews. The Pella mentioned above is situated on the eastern edge of the Jordan rift, opposite the bay of Beth-Shean (42). It played a special role in the history of primitive Christianity. It was to Pella that the original Christian community of Jerusalem fled before the beginning of the first Jewish rebellion against the Romans (66–70 A.D.). Pella was not involved in this rebellion. The photograph shows the valley of the Wadi Jirm el-Moz, which runs down to the plain of Jordan. In the background are the West Jordan mountains. Pella was situated on the ridge that extends into the picture on the right.

Between the Yarmuk and the Jabbok stretches the territory called the Ajlun, which has a considerable stand of forest, though it is not so dense as our German forests. But to eyes accustomed now to barren surfaces the bright green of pines (and some oaks) comes as a surprise and a delight.

■

The site of Gerasa (Jerash today) in the southeast of the Ajlun is impressive because of its tremendous remains from the Roman period (44–46). Jerash was settled very early; some Bronze Age remains have been discovered. In Hellenistic times the settlement grew in importance; the name "Antioch," which for a time supplanted the Semitic name Gerasa, could refer to its founder, the Seleucid ruler Antiochus IV. (This "Antioch" is not to be confused with the Hellenistic metropolis of the same name near the mouth of the Orontes, which gained importance in the early history of the church—cf. Acts 11:19 ff.) The city flourished particularly in the Roman period, and especially in the first and second centuries after Christ.

A Roman architect devised a comprehensive design for the city, the

Forum and Colonnaded Street

ground plan of which is set by the axis of a colonnade, crossed by two streets at right angles. For the first time in this book we encounter a colonnade, as we shall again in the Jerusalem of Hadrian's time and the Palmyra of the age of the Caesars. Colonnades are the representative shopping streets of this period. Whole columns of quarrymen, stonecutters, and masons must have been at work here. At the southern entrance is an arch of triumph with three gates which was erected in honor of Emperor Hadrian. In the winter of 129–130 A.D. he came to visit the city and remained for some time. The first photograph (44) gives us a view of the colonnaded forum, which is shaped like a horseshoe, or better, an ellipse.

The mile-and-a-half-long colonnaded street is still covered with its original pavement, in which the marks of the chariot wheels, cut like a track, are visible (as in Roman Pompeii.). A broad staircase (45) leads from the colonnade to the temple of Artemis. The great columns of this temple

have defied the storms of time, whereas many of the columns of the shopping street were demolished by the Circassians, who were settled on the east side of the valley by the Turks near the end of the last century.

On the south side of the city lies one of its two theaters (46), containing thirty-two rows of seats and capable of accommodating about five thousand spectators. Though it is small compared with other similar theaters

45 Jerash:
     Staircase to the Temple of Artemis

(the one in Ephesus mentioned in Acts 19:29 held over twenty-five thousand people), it is amazingly well preserved and its acoustics are excellent. You can test the acoustics for yourself. Standing in the semicircular stage (in the immediate foreground of the photograph), you can speak in a low voice and still be easily heard in the top row. Some of the demolished back wall of the stage still remains. The king of Jordan, Hussein II, is

46 Jerah: Theater

restoring the theater, as the colonnaded portico, the Stoa of Attalos, has

been restored in Athens. Thus it is easy to imagine how it all looked ori-

ginally, though one may have some misgivings about such reconstructions.

In the Christian era Jerash has had a large Christian community. During

the course of the centuries many churches took the place of the temple.

No fewer than eleven churches go back to the fifth and sixth centuries.   47 Valley of the Jabbok

The Jabbok could not be omitted from our series of pictures (47). It has a good flow of water the year round. Its banks are bordered by oleander bushes with their pink flowers. On the other side of the stream a plowman is driving a furrow through the land, probably with a wooden plow. The oxen yoked to the plow are clearly discernible. It must be noted here that the processes of sowing and plowing remain much the same as they were thousands of years ago, as is also the case with threshing and winnowing. In the next picture we see a large village threshing floor with a boy riding back and forth on a threshing board until all the grain is threshed out (48). Then when the wind is blowing the grain and the chaff are pitched up with a winnowing fan and the chaff flies away. How many metaphors and parables in the Bible reflect the everyday life of the farmer: the sowing and the harvest, the threshing and winnowing, the gathering

48 Threshing Scene
    at a Village Threshing Floor

into barns! "The kingdom of God is as if a man should scatter seed upon the ground, and should sleep and rise night and day, and the seed should sprout and grow, he knows not how. The earth produces of itself, first the blade, then the ear, then the full grain in the ear. But when the grain is ripe, at once he puts in the sickle, because the harvest has come" (Mark 4:26–29).

Or again in the most familiar of all the parables of this kind, the parable of the Sower: "Listen! A sower went out to sow. And as he sowed, some seed fell along the path, and the birds came and devoured it. Other seed fell on rocky ground, where it had not much soil, and immediately it sprang up, since it had no depth of soil; and when the sun rose it was scorched, and since it had no root it withered away. Other seed fell among thorns and the thorns grew up and choked it, and it yielded no grain. And other seeds fell into good soil and brought forth grain, growing up and increasing and yielding thirtyfold and sixtyfold and a hundredfold.' And he said, 'He who has ears to hear, let him hear' " (Mark 4:3–9).

In the Old Testament the same everyday events are used parabolically:
"Does he who plows for sowing plow continually?
    does he continually open and harrow his ground?
When he has leveled its surface
    does he not scatter dill, sow cummin,
and put in wheat in rows
    and barley in its proper place,
    and spelt as the border:
For he is instructed aright;
    his God teaches him.
Dill is not threshed with a threshing sledge,
    nor is a cart wheel rolled over cummin;
    but dill is beaten out with a stick,

and cummin with a rod.

Does one crush bread grain?

No, he does not thresh it for ever;

When he drives his cart wheel over it

with his horses, he does not crush it.

This also comes from the Lord of hosts;

49   Tell of Penuel in Jabbok Valley

> he is wonderful in counsel,
>
> and excellent in wisdom." (Isa. 28:24–29)

Thus God does everything in his time.

In the year 1908 a small limestone tablet was found at Gezer on which was inscribed an ancient farmer's calendar, giving a list of the various months and the agricultural work done in them: "Two months of ingathering. Two months of sowing. Two months of late planting. Month of pulling flax. Month of barley harvest. Month when everything else is harvested. Two months of vine-tending. Month of summer-fruit." This agricultural calendar may go as far back as the tenth century before Christ. The enumeration begins with the month of October.

For the farmer the year begins with the change from the rainy to the dry season. The photographs in this book were all taken toward the end of the dry season, before the fall of the first rains. This should be remembered in noting the lack of color in the pictures. They show the Palestinian landscape between August and October. The landscape begins to change with the coming of the so-called early rains (October–November). Then appears the tender green of the grasses, and soon the crocus, clematis, narcissus, and other field flowers spring up. In the course of the rainy season, especially in the spring, they cover the slopes and valleys with a prodigal abundance of blooms:

> "The flowers appear on the earth,
>
> the time of singing has come,
>
> and the voice of the turtledove is heard in our land.
>
> The fig tree puts forth its figs,
>
> and the vines are in blossom . . ." (Song of Sol. 2:12 f.).

The late rains conclude the rainy season (in April); so the general rule is: "Six months of summer and six months of rain." For the Palestinian the year has only two long seasons, as is indicated in the passage that proclaims the creative goodness of God: "While the earth remains, seedtime

and harvest, cold and heat, summer and winter, day and night, shall not cease'' (Gen. 8:22).

We return to the Jabbok and follow it upstream. On the way we pass many grazing flocks of small cattle, sheep, and goats, driven by whistling herders. Shortly before the Jabbok valley narrows for the first time, we turn a bend in the road and see before us the tell of Penuel (49). This is the place referred to by the Old Testament narrator as the spot where Jacob's flocks crossed over the Jabbok (Gen. 32). Jacob is moved by the blessings he has received: "O Lord . . . , I am not worthy of the least of all the steadfast love and all the faithfulness which thou hast shown to thy servant, for with only my staff I crossed this Jordan; and now I have be-

50   Plain North of the Road from
       Amman to Es-Salt

come two companies . . ." But Jacob is afraid of the meeting with his brother Esau that lies ahead of him. And so he sends a great present to him, flocks of sheep and goats, asses, cows, and camels: "Perhaps he will accept me." Even at this point we sense a great tension in the story. But during the nocturnal crossing of the Jabbok comes the breathtaking event which every Bible reader knows: Jacob's wrestling with God. If hitherto the prospect of meeting his brother weighed heavily upon his mind, now he is confronted with a quite different affliction by his encounter with God. In the face of this trial all the other burdens that press upon Jacob pale into insignificance. And here the story opens up and gathers into itself the experiences which Israel had with its God again and again throughout its history—experiences of extreme judgment and extreme grace. And "the sun rose upon him as he passed Penuel."

A ravine leads from the tell of Penuel up to the tell of Mahanaim. The

51 Plateau Southwest of Amman
    Not Far from Heshbon

82

Midianites who were smitten by Gideon on the Plain of Jezreel would have left the valley of the Jabbok here on their flight over the "caravan route" (Judg. 8:11), using the ravine and, as they continued their retreat, touching the plain of El-Bukea, north of the road from Amman to Es-Salt (Martin Noth). The evening light brings out the forms of the landscape with unusual power and clarity (50).

52 View from the Tell of Heshbon
    to the North

83

South of Amman, the present residence of the king of Jordan, stretches a broad, fertile tableland, which is intersected by the Arnon River and was in ancient times inhabited by the Moabites. The Israelite kings were reaching out for this granary. At the time when Israel was ruled by the house of Omri (I Kings 16:16 ff.) an energetic Moabite king named Mesha succeeded in throwing off his vassalage to Israel. He gives an account of his campaigns in an inscription upon a stele erected by him (the so-called Moabite Stone, which was discovered in Dibon in 1868): "I saw my desire upon him and upon his house, when Israel perished utterly for ever." Mesha was able to extend the territory of the Moabites considerably to the north and also to incorporate in it, among others, the city of Medeba.

Our photographs show the plateau with its fertile fields (51—52). The ground has already been largely cultivated and is now waiting for the

53 Byzantine Basilica on Ras Siaghah

84

rains to come. Near Aroer (the modern 'Ara 'ir) the Arnon has entrenched itself some 2,100 feet into the plateau, which continues beyond the fissured valley (54). This is a clear illustration of the tableland character of the landscape. The upper edges of the valley are about two and a half miles apart at this point. The ruins in the foreground of photograph 52 are remains of the Roman-Byzantine Heshbon, which we are familiar with from

54 Valley of the Arnon

85

the Old Testament tradition. In Roman times a Roman road followed the track of an ancient thoroughfare from the Jordan rift by way of Heshbon to the East Jordan plateau.

On the elevation called Ras Siaghah, not far from Mount Nebo, lies a Byzantine basilica, the ground plan of which is fairly discernible in our photograph (53). It was erected in 597 A.D., after a smaller, older church had been destroyed (supposedly by an earthquake). In the lower right-hand corner of the picture one can see the remains of a mosaic pavement (with representations of animals), which is characteristic of the Byzantine churches and which we shall encounter again in another unusually significant example (56).

But before we come to this let us say a brief word concerning the site of the Byzantine church just mentioned. We find ourselves on a height about 3,500 feet above the Dead Sea, directly east of the mouth of the river Jordan, which is about ten miles away. In clear weather the view extends from Hebron over the Olivet range at Jerusalem and the hill country of Samaria to Mount Carmel and Mount Hermon. Unfortunately, we did not get this view. However, we did see the Dead Sea and the Jordan rift, the course of the Jordan itself being clearly marked by the dark brushwood on its bank. Otherwise a curtain of haze erased the outlines of the landscape, permitting only very subdued colors to come through. According to the Old Testament, it may have been from here that Moses looked out over the Promised Land, which it was not granted to him to enter.

∎∎

The concluding section of this sequence of pictures is also intended to be a prelude to a shorter series of photographs of Jerusalem. In a Byzantine church in Madeba (55) some fascinating remains of a mosaic pavement of the end of the sixth century, depicting a map of Palestine, have been preserved. Madeba itself, which is mentioned in the Moabite Stone inscription, but also in the Old Testament (cf. Josh. 13:9; Isa. 15:2; Chron. 19:7),

55 Madeba from the South

is situated on a small elevation southeast of Ras Siaghah. With its flat-roofed, one-story houses, it presents the typical picture of a Palestinian settlement. Incidentally, the Byzantine church is situated on the side of the elevation which is not visible in our picture.

The brilliantly executed mosaic map (considering the difficulty of working with this material) covers a considerable geographical area. The fragments which have survived extend from Shechem or the mouth of the Jabbok River to the Nile delta. We present here only one section, a map of Jerusalem (56). The artist gave it special priority, as is indicated by the enormous scale with which Jerusalem is rendered in relation to the rest of the map. The plan of the city (like the rest of the Madeba map) is "oriented" from west to east.

We cannot here go into the history of Jerusalem, but it must be remarked that this astonishingly exact picture of the city, which shows the ground plan of the Christian-Byzantine city at the end of the sixth century, is based upon the network of streets established in Hadrian's Roman colony Aelia Capitolina. The foundation of the Roman colony goes back to Emperor Hadrian, who also carried it out after the military suppression of the second Jewish rebellion (132–135 A.D.). This was intended to write finis to the history of Israel. Henceforth, no Jew was allowed to enter the holy city. Jerusalem became a Roman provincial city like others, with Roman style, Roman military, and Roman temples. Thus on the old temple site, on which the Temple of Solomon had stood, there now arose the temple of Jupiter Capitolinus. Even the former name of the Roman province, Judea, was extinguished and replaced with the term Palestine.

In our mosaic map of the city a great colonnaded street stands out as the north-south axis of the city. Eusebius speaks of it as the "middle market street." The north gate (on the site of the present Damascus Gate) is especially emphasized, but other gates are also clearly marked. A second colonnaded street running east of the main axis immediately strikes the eye.

The columns are shown in vertical position, as the gates and towers are also depicted in non-perspective form, and the map as a whole uses both the plane and perspective style of representation (Carl Watzinger). Closer examination will show that topographically a large number of buildings have been indicated. We mention only the Church of the Holy Sepulcher (between the middle of the main axis and the west gate of the city). "Details which can be clearly seen are the open court with its flight of steps in the east, the atrium with its three gates, the basilica of the Martyrium or the basilica of Constantine, and the dome of the Anastasis" (Peter Thomsen). These are not difficult to recognize in our photograph. Thus the master artist who designed the mosaic map constructed this picture of "the holy city of Jerusalem" (as the Greek letters call it) with great care and skill, while the map as a whole indicates the hand of an artist and a well-conceived plan both in its design and in its coloring.

56   Madeba: Mosaic Map

Between the Jerusalem of the Madeba map and the Jerusalem of today
(57) lies another long and troubled span of history, covering almost a
millennium and a half, which we cannot go into here. But the historian,
even if he wishes to limit himself strictly to the history of the city, must
always take into account the broad historical connections. As everyone
knows, this imperative applies also to the present-day divided city of Jerusalem, the old city of which belongs to Jordan, while the western part is
the seat of the government of the state of Israel. A small strip of no-
man's-land runs through the middle of Jerusalem; this provisional boundary line like the whole boundary between the two states is nothing more
than an armistice line. But when will there ever be real peace here?

If one drives from Jericho to Jerusalem, the heights of the Mount of Olives
range can be seen very soon, even before the road ascends and takes

57 Jerusalem from the Mount of Olives

its serpentine path across the Desert of Judah. But only when the southern slope of the range has been passed does the city suddenly appear palpably near, a view that never ceases to be overwhelming. One can feel even today the exultation of the Psalm:

" 'Our feet have been standing

within your gates, O Jerusalem!

Peace be within your walls,

and security within your towers!'

For my brethren and companions' sake

I will say, 'Peace be within you!'

For the sake of the house of the Lord our God,

I will seek your good." (Ps. 122:2, 7–9)

58 Jerusalem: Herod's Gate

Our picture was taken from the slope of the Mount of Olives. Dominating the center of the picture is the Temple area (Haram esh-Sherif) with the Dome of the Rock and its high cupola and the El-Aksa mosque on the south side (on the left edge of the picture). Between the city and the Mount of Olives lies the valley of the Kidron, which at this point is not very deep. The Temple area is astonishingly extensive and our photograph gives some impression of this fact. To illustrate this I give its dimensions. The east side, facing us, 1,528 feet long, the west side 1,600 feet. The shorter sides measure 1,017 feet on the north and 918 feet on the south. It is thus an irregular rectangle of great amplitude. This expanded plan goes back to Herod the Great, who enlarged the area to almost double its former extent. The expansion caused the architects no little trouble, since the southeast corner of the Temple area (at the left edge of the picture) rises 154 feet above the bedrock. Tremendous supporting vaults over the foundation had to be erected here, and these can still be seen if one goes down the steps that lead underneath the Temple area.

So again we encounter the great builder, Herod (cf. 33, 36, 37, 39). The Temple of Jerusalem was his greatest architectural achievement. Only small remnants of it have survived. The Temple itself, as is well known, was completely destroyed in the conquest of the city in 70 A.D. by the general and subsequently emperor Titus. There are, however, a few remains of the enclosure wall of the Temple area—for example, part of the so-called Wailing Wall at which the Jews lamented the destruction of the Temple. (Despite the provisions of the armistice agreement, it is inaccessible to the Jews today.) One still stands in admiration today before these huge, carefully hewn blocks of stone, which are typical of the Herodian masonry. Mark the Evangelist says: "And as he came out of the temple, one of his disciples said to him. 'Look, Teacher, what wonderful stones and what wonderful buildings!' And Jesus said to him, 'Do you see these great buildings? There will not be left here one stone upon another, that will not be thrown down'" (Mark 13:1–2).

59 Dome of the Rock: Southern Entrance

Besides the Temple, Herod built a mighty palace guarded by towers and the Castle of Antonia at the northwest corner of the Temple area. The Roman governor, Pontius Pilate, would have resided in the king's palace when he was in Jerusalem. This stood in the neighborhood of the present Jaffa Gate, directly upon the boundary line between Jordan and Israel, which can be crossed only at the Gate of Gennath. In our picture (57) a strip (in the west) is already a part of the state of Israel.

We enter Jerusalem through Herod's Gate (58). The city wall is of a later date. It stems from the Turkish period, though its foundations are older. A great deal of traffic flows through the gate and even more through the Damascus Gate. The interior of the city is often tremendously crowded— not surprising when one remembers that the streets and lanes are narrow, as they were in ancient times. Heavily laden donkeys are driven with

60 Dome of the Rock:
Row of Columns

loud cries through the swarming streets by energetic drivers. Watersellers offer their precious commodity, making themselves heard by crashing together two brass bowls. Naturally, you can also get Turkish coffee, which you drink from tiny cups. If you are hungry, you can buy small bread cakes or try some fresh roasted peanuts. From the carts which are shoved about the streets you can buy almost everything you would find in a regular store: wonderful fruits and all kinds of vegetables, handmade leather and metal goods, and even woodcarvings, such as Nativity figurines made of olivewood. Squatting behind their boxes are the shoeshine boys. They are true masters of their trade, and under their ministrations the dustiest shoes are made to shine like new. People from all over the globe come streaming by. The Arabs wear both Bedouin and European dress. Almost every faith is represented in the streets. If you are recognized as a tourist,

61   Dome of the Rock: Windows

95

guides of all ages dog your steps, offering to conduct the stranger through the maze of streets to his destination, and it is not always easy to shake them off. The Jerusalem of today very largely presents the picture of an Oriental city.

The Dome of the Rock (59—61) is, of course, easy to find if one is walking south from Herod's Gate. It was built in the years 687–691, in the reign of the Ummayyad caliph, Abd al-Malik, over the sacred rock on which Solomon's temple also was built. The ground plan has the form of a regular octagon. The brilliant glazed brickwork (from Tabriz in Persia) was installed later by Sultan Solyman the Magnificent (1520–1566). Perhaps any attempt to describe this most important monument of early Islamic art in Palestine is unnecessary. The windows shown in photograph 61 can also be seen on the right of photograph 60. The large picture (59) shows the southern entrance.

If we leave Jerusalem from the east at St. Stephen's Gate (62), the Valley of Kidron lies before us. On the other side rises the Mount of Olives with the olive trees that give it its name. Here too is the Garden of Gethsemane (63) which is so carefully tended by the Franciscans. Farther up is the Russian Orthodox garden. Our photograph shows ancient olive trees in the midst of brilliant bloom. Looking back one sees again the enclosure wall of the Temple area with the Golden Gate (near the right edge of photograph 57) and above it the cupola of the Dome of the Rock. Here one is far removed from the hustle and bustle of the city; the Gethsemane story comes alive and makes one forget all the superficialities. Even the human actors in the Passion story recede into the background and the Cross of Christ becomes the cup which the Father cannot spare his Son: "Abba, Father, all things are possible to thee; remove this cup from me; yet not what I will, but what thou wilt" (Mark 14:36). In the Gethsemane story the whole event becomes something that happens between the Father and the Son. Jesus is not subject to the inescapable fatality of

62 St. Stephen's Gate

96

history, the irresistible consequences of conditions. His way to the Cross is obedience to the will of the Father. This is the secret of his Cross as the Gethsemane story tells it — and tells it without eliminating or diminishing the guilty part men played in crucifying him, for while these words were being uttered in the Garden of Gethsemane Judas was already on his way to betray his Lord.

For us Jerusalem means, beyond all the vicissitudes of its troubled history, the story of Jesus of Nazareth, his Cross, and his resurrection.

We present here a few pictures of the site on the northwest shore of the Dead Sea where the Qumran texts were discovered. These texts are still in the process of publication and are just beginning to be evaluated. There can be no question, however, of their importance for Old Testament and even more for New Testament studies. Indeed, that importance increases the more carefully the texts are studied. Here a whole library has been rescued from oblivion: Old Testament texts more than a thousand years older than our oldest manuscripts; late Jewish writings, some known as well as others hitherto unknown; commentaries on books of the Bible; and finally, the regulations, hymns, and prayers of a pre-Christian, late Jewish community. In addition the remains of the settlement of this com-

munity have been excavated. An extensive complex of buildings includes, among others, a great hall (seventy-two feet long), in which the people met for communal meals and meetings, baths for the daily immersions, cisterns for the water supply, workshops (mill, bakery, pottery, smithy), a room containing writing tables, benches, and inkwells, storerooms, and

63 Garden of Gethsemane

99

so on. The texts were found in caves, some near and some farther away from the settlement.

We drive down from Jerusalem on the Jericho Road to the Dead Sea. Soon we are in the uninhabited wilderness of the Desert of Judah (64). Only now and then do we meet a donkey rider or a shepherd with a tiny flock, which must be content with the scantiest of pasture here. This is the setting of the parable of the Good Samaritan (Luke 10:30–37). Here the man who was on his way from Jerusalem to Jericho fell among robbers and was left beaten and helpless on the roadside. Two things join to set the scene of the parable: this lonely road is a perfect place for an ambush, and, on the other hand, there was nobody for miles around who could help the stricken man. And yet "by chance" a priest and a Levite came down the road. But they detoured around him and passed by. Was

64 Ancient Jericho Road

it simply the place itself and the lonely surroundings that struck fear into them and quickened their pace, so that there is no need to ask for further reasons? They acted on the principle that every man is his own neighbor. Who could guarantee that they would not suffer the same fate that overtook this man? And then again "by chance" another man came by, and he

65 Monastery of St. George
    in the Wadi Kelt

101

gave help — the miracle of neighborliness, though he did nothing more than what we could. But he made use of his possibilities, and that is what counts. And so there eventuated what the scene cries out for: love.

I believe that our photograph of the scenery does help us to understand the parable better, even though scenery is not often emphasized in the parables. In his exegesis of this story Adolf Schlatter observed that the scenery strengthens the graphic "plasticity" of the parable as he also emphasized the freedom with which the parable was formed in order to bring out its message. According to his exposition, "the teaching value of the narrative lies in the fact that on both sides the figures are so constructed that it is unambiguously clear what love is. The wounded man whom Jesus sets down in the desert between Jerusalem and Jericho is the man who needs help. . . . Jesus put the Samaritan in the parable in order to strip the lifeless term 'neighbor' of its dead formalism and make it live." For Schlatter the priest and the Levite become "contrasting figures" (Das Evangelium des Lukas, 1931, p. 286). It is precisely when we see this element of conscious structuring in the parable, as Schlatter does, that the scenery takes on its illuminative significance.

The loneliness and desolation of the landscape between Jerusalem and the Jordan rift can also be seen in the next photograph (65). Set into the steep cliff above the deep gorge of the Wadi Kelt is the Greek Orthodox monastery of St. George, almost completely cut off from the surrounding world, like the monastery of Mar Saba to the south on the Wadi en-Nar. Impressive for me was a flight over the desert of Judah at a relatively low altitude from which I saw the frequently traveled route from Jerusalem to Jericho. Every turn in the road was long since familiar to me and easily recognized. The shadow of the plane glided slowly over the ground beneath which looked like frozen waves of a heavy sea. The oasis of Jericho stood out as clearly as the north shore of the Dead Sea. In innumerable loops the Jordan approached its mouth.

66   The Jordan

The Jordan! One always thinks of it as being larger than it really is (66).
Nor does it have a fertile plain on both sides as one might suppose.
Rather, beyond a small strip of green undergrowth on its banks lies a
broad expanse of marl that resembles a lunar landscape, with strange
table-shaped mounds of a gray-white color on which nothing grows. The
reason is that the Jordan is a deep gully, from which the water would
have to be elevated in order to irrigate the Jordan rift.

The Jordan is connected with the name of John the Baptist, his call to re-
pentance and his baptism for the remission of sins. The bold figure of
John stands at the beginning of the Gospels: "And there went out to him
all the country of Judea, and all the people of Jerusalem; and they were
baptized by him in the river Jordan, confessing their sins" (Mark 1:5).
Among the many John baptized was he the thong of whose sandals he

67 Northwest Shore of the Dead Sea

104

68　Roland de Vaux,
　　the Archeologist (at right)

felt unworthy to unloose. Our photograph shows the Jordan at one of the places where tradition says that John baptized.

Quickly we reach the northwest shore of the Dead Sea (67). Its blue surface stretches far to the south, not a monotonous blue but surprisingly varied in shading. In the foreground the rock of Ras Feshka projects into the picture. Nearby is a spring the waters of which taste somewhat sulphurous. This is where the Qumran community did its farming and if we turn west at a right angle on the spot from which the picture was taken we see less than three-quarters of a mile away the ruins of the ancient settlement of Qumran situated on a marl terrace some seventy-five feet high (69). The marl terrace is immediately in front of the steep slope of the West Jordan mountains. In the rainy season a stream comes down from the cliff wall, near the center of the picture, the water of which was care-

fully stored in Qumran. Also in the middle of the picture some of the remains of the buildings being excavated can be seen. The water of the Wadi Qumran ran to the settlement through an aqueduct or series of canals, still discernible today. As is well known, the water of the Dead Sea cannot be used by man or beast. It is so full of salt and minerals that no organic life can survive in it. Its salt content is five times that of the Atlantic. The artist who designed the Madeba map (56) shows two fish meeting not far from the mouth of the Jordan. One fish is returning from the Dead Sea, pushing its way up the Jordan, and seems to be telling the other fish that there is nothing for either of them in the Dead Sea.

We insert here a photograph of the distinguished excavator of Qumran, the French Dominican father Roland de Vaux (68). With an expert eye he examines the day's yield of potsherds being presented to him by an as-

69   Marl Terrace of Qumran

sistant. This scene, which took place during an excavating campaign at Tell el-Farah, is typical of all archeological work (cf. 32).

The history of the discovery of Qumran is not without it adventurous side. In the spring of 1947, Bedouins who were searching for a lost goat stumbled upon the first cave, which contained seven leather scrolls (70). This

70 Qumran: Cave I

107

was the beginning of a whole series of finds. Especially rich was Cave IV, which was discovered in a marl strip in the immediate vicinity of the settlement, again by Bedouins (71). It was constructed by human hands and had been inhabited. Traces of soot on the walls point to the use of oil lamps. A view from a "window" of the cave looks across the Dead Sea to the East Jordan mountains (72). In Cave IV the Bedouins picked up fragments of over three hundred individual manuscripts, among them portions of all the books of the Old Testament excepting the book of Esther. Especially abundant were parts of Isaiah and Deuteronomy. Besides biblical texts and commentaries (always in fragments) there were portions of apocalyptic, paraenetical, and liturgical writings. Some of the very small scraps of leather must be laboriously pieced together, which work, of course, entails large gaps.

Along with the smaller fragments, large consecutive texts were also found. The best known are the scrolls from Cave I (for example, two Isaiah scrolls, the Manual of Discipline, the thanksgiving hymns, etc.). These scrolls were stored in pottery jars of the same size and form as others which were later discovered on the grounds of the settlement, evidence of the connection between the texts and the inhabitants of the settlement. It was an ancient custom to store documents which one wished to preserve in pottery jars. Thus, for example, the prophet Jeremiah directs Baruch to take deeds of purchase for a field in Anathoth, after they had been signed by witnesses, and preserve them in "an earthenware vessel, that they may last for a long time" (Jer. 32:14).

According to the pottery and coins discovered here, the settlement was first inhabited in the period between 130 and 31 B.C. and then again from 4 B.C. to 68 A.D. by a late Jewish sectarian community (de Vaux). This means that the manuscripts were buried in the caves at the latest toward

the end of the second period in order to preserve them from the clutches of the Roman legions which were approaching for the siege of Jerusalem. This dating in itself indicates that the biblical texts of Qumran are highly important for the new insights they provide into the history of the text of the Old Testament. Equally valuable is the enrichment of our knowledge

71 Qumran: Cave IV

of late Judaism, though we still cannot see all the historical connections. The very fact that the somewhat uniform impression of late Judaism which one can get from the rabbinical tradition is now corrected by one that has many more levels is important enough. The Order of Qumran (naturally, this designation must not be pressed) regarded itself as the elect holy remnant of Israel and the "congregation of the new covenant." It went beyond the Pharisaic movement in the strictness of its interpretation of the Torah. It aimed to "prepare the way of the Lord in the wilderness" (Isa. 40:3) and lived in expectation of the imminent end of all history. Its Rule shows that it had an extremely strict organization. The pious men of Qumran believed that they were summoned to a holy war, to be God's shock troops, constantly challenged to oppose the world and sin. In addition to the smaller circle of the order which lived the communal life in Qumran, there were "lay brotherhoods" scattered about the country.

We select here, in order to provide at least a glimpse into the Qumran texts, a sample from the so-called "Book of Hymns" (1 QH), as it has been called since the texts were first published by E. L. Sukenik. Only fragments have been preserved.

"I give thanks unto Thee, O Lord, for Thou hast put my soul in the bundle of life and hedged me against all the snares of corruption. . . . Verily I know that righteousness lies not with man, nor perfection of conduct with mortals. Only with God on high are all works of righteousness; and ne'er can the way of man be stablished save by the spirit which God has fashioned for him, to bring unto perfection the life of mortal man; that all His works may know how mighty is His power, how plenteous His love to all who do His will. When I called to mind all my guilty deeds and the perfidy of my sires . . . trembling seized hold on me and quaking, all my bones were a-quiver; my heart became like wax melting before a fire, my

knees were like to water pouring over a steep. . . . But then, when I re-membered the strength of Thy hand and Thy multitudinous mercies, I rose again and stood upright. . . . For Thou wilt wipe out all sin, in Thy bounty it lies to purify man from guilt. Man alone cannot do as Thou hast done; for Thou didst create both the righteous and the wicked. . . . What is man,

72 Qumran: View from Cave IV

mere earth, kneaded out of [clay], destined to return unto the dust, that Thou shouldst give him insight into Thy wonders and make him privy to things divine? As for me, I am but dust and ashes. What can I devise except Thou hast desired it? And what can I think apart from Thy will? And how be strong except Thou hast stayed me, or stumbled except Thou hast constrained me? How speak except Thou hast opened my mouth? How reply except Thou hast given me sense? Lo, Thou art the Prince of the angels, and the King of all that are in glory, and the Lord of every spirit, and the Ruler of every deed. Without Thee nothing is wrought, and without Thy will can nothing be known. None there is beside Thee, and none to share Thy power, and none to match Thy glory, and Thy power is beyond price. Which among all Thy wondrous work has power to stand before Thee? How much less, then, can be who returns to his dust attain

73 Oasis of Damascus

to [such power]? Only for Thine own glory hast Thou done all these things."

We add a few lines from the Manual of Discipline (1 QS): "For He, in His compassion, has drawn me near to Him, and His judgment upon me shall be rendered in His mercy. In His bounteous truth He has judged me, and in

His abundant goodness will shrive my iniquities, and in His righteousness
cleanse me from all the pollution of man and the sin of human kind, that
I may acknowledge unto God His righteousness, and unto the Most High
His majestic splendor." (Translation by Theodor H. Gaster.)

The devout men of Qumran are not mentioned in the New Testament.
This may be surprising, for the Pharisees and Sadducees are often spoken
of, — indeed, on almost every page of the Gospels. Were the relationships of primitive Palestinian Christianity closer to them than to the Pharisees and Sadducees? The relation of the Qumran community (which in
all probability is identical with the Essenic movement known to us through
Philo and Josephus) to the New Testament needs to be carefully investi-
gated. It is still too early to make a final judgment. What is emerging
more and more clearly is an abundance of likenesses but even more fun-

75 Palmyra: Colonnade

114

damental differences. But this we cannot go into here, since it would require detailed comparison of the texts, which would take us far beyond the bounds of this book.

Two short sequences of pictures form the conclusion of this book. They lead us to the Euphrates and the Nile. Once more we recall the broad horizon in which the Bible history belongs. Thus the beginning and the

76 Palmyra: View to the Castle

end of the book correspond.

Naturally, here we are obliged even more than usual to be content with
suggestions. And besides, what should be said here can be conveyed by
picture only in a limited sense. We have already mentioned Israel's encounter with the world of religion which it found when it entered Palestine.
That world was made very real for us in the texts of Ugarit. But throughout its history in every contact with the great political powers Israel also
encountered the gods of these powers. Recall the scene that took place
outside the wall of Jerusalem when it was besieged by Sennacherib. The
spokesman of the Assyrian king speaks provocatively to the people who
are listening from the wall:

"Do not listen to Hezekiah when he misleads you by saying, The Lord
will deliver us. Has any of the gods of the nations ever delivered his land
out of the hand of the king of Assyria? Where are the gods of Hamath and

Arpad? Where are the gods of Sepharvaim. Hena, and Ivvah? Have they

delivered Samaria out of my hand? Who among all the gods of the

countries have delivered their countries out of my hand, that the Lord

should deliver Jerusalem out of my hand?" (II Kings 18:32–35).

So the "world" with which Israel had to deal in its history always was the

world of religions too. In the face of this world Israel had to preserve its

faith. Therefore the concluding part of this book is concerned with the

environment of Israel (and early Christianity) in the broadest sense, even

though the inclusion of the temple of the gods of Palmyra and the temples

of the Pharaohs of Egypt can only be intended to serve as examples.

Among the titles of the Pharaohs was the designation "The Good God,"

since the Pharaohs were regarded as incarnations of the divinity. It is no

78 Palmyra: Temple of Baal-Shamin

accident that in Israel the institution of kingship did not come until rather late, and the mythical elevation of the king that was customary in Egypt never occurred. Israel's king was a man with all his humanness. The Old Testament never suppressed this fact. So the conflict of early Christianity with the Imperium Romanum on this point was preceded by a long history.

■

Let us briefly orientate ourselves upon the map. In antiquity there were a number of caravan lines between the Mediterranean coast and Mesopotamia. A northerly route went around the desert by way of Aleppo to the great bend of the Euphrates. This was the longest route. We chose the shorter caravan route, which ran in a northeasterly direction from Damascus across the Syrian Desert to the Euphrates. It had the advantage of passing Palmyra at the halfway mark, 143 miles from Damascus and 137 miles from the Euphrates at Dura-Europos. Palmyra, an oasis in the midst of the desert, was a natural "caravan haven" and was important very early, though it did not reach its peak until the first post-Christian centuries.

We left Damascus early in the morning and went northward to Homs (the ancient Emesa) in order to follow the pipeline. Damascus itself is a great oasis on the edge of the desert (73). Its oasis character strikes one immediately as one approaches Damascus by air. The pale gray center of the city is surrounded by a green ring of gardens and fields, beyond which the yellowish-brown desert region begins. The drive across the desert was a long one. Actually, there is no road at all. We followed a line of stakes and a wagon track, making rather slow progress (74). But after all, the 1912 Baedeker estimated that the trip from Damascus to Palmyra and back would require nine whole days. How long would it have taken the camel caravans of ancient times? Today we are losing our sense of distances. By air, the trip can easily be made in one day with plenty of time to see Palmyra itself.

79 Palmyra: Valley of Mortuary Towers

The desert is quite unexpectedly beautiful and colorful. Erhart Kästner advisedly headed his book (Zeltbuch von Tumilad) with the words "Everybody needs some desert." The idea that the desert is boring is completely wrong. Throughout the whole day clouds were to be seen. Their shadows raced over the broad planes and gave movement to the scenery, creating ever-changing contrasts. Smaller and larger elevations accompanied us on both sides, interrupting the great horizontal level where the eye loses itself in infinite distances. Nor is the desert absolutely barren, as one might think. Again and again traces of vegetation appear, coarse grasses and low thornbushes. We passed grazing camels feeding upon this desert growth. Soon after sundown the wind began to whistle in from the west, and during a moonlit night it grew downright cold in contrast with the heat of the day.

Early the next morning the whole terrain of ancient Palmyra was bathed in brilliant sunshine. First to impress us was the colonnaded street (75). It was no less than a mile long and about thirty-six feet wide. It consisted originally of about 375 Corinthian columns, of which 150 are still standing. In our picture we can clearly see the projecting brackets on which stood the figures of the founder and honored citizens of the city, probably officers, wealthy caravan merchants, and bankers. Their names are given in inscriptions carved in the Palmyrene script, in which the Aramaic language, spoken in Palmyra along with the Greek language, was written. Palmyra is reminiscent in many ways of Gerasa, since the buildings of both cities are fairly contemporary. Emperor Hadrian, whose favor Gerasa enjoyed, also visited and promoted Palmyra. The colonnade runs in a curve to the great temple of Bel (77). If the area of the columned court is included, it covers a square that measures 590 feet on each side. The base of Cologne Cathedral would fit into this nine times. We climbed to the roof and looked out over modern Palmyra, the plan of which is so regular that it looks as if it had been laid out on a drawing board. It was

built to accommodate the Bedouins who lived in the ruins of the temple court when the French mandate government resettled them in 1929 in order to free the ancient city for research and the tourists.

The temple reflects the relations that Palmyra had with the east. Bel is a Babylonian god. Especially well preserved is the small temple of Baal-Shamin (78), but here the name of the god would indicate a western origin, since the term "lord of heaven" is of Phoenician origin. In addition an almost innumerable profusion of gods of the most diverse origins were worshiped, including other Babylonian as well as Arabian, Greek, and Roman gods and native Palmyrene gods. Otto Eissfeldt has suggested that Bel is only a renamed god who originally bore the name of a Palmyrene god.

The valley of mortuary towers (79) runs from east to west. About 150 such

80 Palmyra: Group of Columns

121

towers, which are typical of Palmyra, are still standing. The rich Palmyrenes buried their dead in them. They can run as much as sixty-five feet in height. The form appears to have developed from one-story mortuaries, which can also be found in Palmyra, along with an underground necropolis containing multiple corridors, rooms, and statues of the dead.

In photograph 71 we see on the heights above Palmyra a post-medieval castle (cf. 76), dating back to the Turkish period. It was built around 1600 A.D. and served to fortify Palmyra, which was still important though it had long since lost its former splendor.

At first the rich remains of this desert city may present something of an enigma. How did such wealth concentrate here? The answer is relatively simple. It was already its location that gave Palmyra its importance. It is mentioned in Babylonian texts (as Tadmor) around 2000 B.C. and later appears frequently in the archives of Mari (of which we shall speak shortly). Tadmor also occurs in the Old Testament (II Chron. 8:4). The Palmyra shown in our pictures is, of course, that of the first Christian centuries. Not until the second half of the third century did it reach its noblest development. And this was connected with the political situation of the Roman Empire at that time.

The great caravan cities were not merely halting places for the caravans but also "clearing houses" (Michael Rostovtzeff) or "transshipment ports." The goods coming from the west were taken over by other caravans going farther east. The more overland caravans that stopped at Palmyra, the more money migrated to Palmyra. At its peak it had become a mighty caravan city which was reaching out for political sovereignty. Odenathus of Palmyra was honored with the title of Imperator by the Romans in 238 A.D. and later, when he had defeated the Persians, given the title of Augustus; and it was the ambition of his widow, Zenobia, to make Palmyra independent. She dared to seize control of Egypt, the granary of Rome. This extraordinary woman herself led the troops of Palmyra on

the campaign. Her plan was to unite the ancient Hellenistic East against Rome (Fritz Taeger). She extended her power as far as Asia Minor, though she did not succeed in taking the Bosporus. Boldly she had coins minted bearing only her image and not equally that of the emperor. She raised herself and her son to the rank of Augustus and Augusta. There could be only one answer: Emperor Aurelian advanced upon Palmyra after having reconquered Egypt. Zenobia took flight but was captured by Aurelian's soldiers just as she was about to board a boat to cross the Euphrates. But we must pass over the details. In 273 A.D. Palmyra was destroyed by the Romans.

81 Palmyra: Columns in Evening Light

We take leave of Palmyra with two photographs. The setting sun bathes

the columns with its colors until they glow with an ever deeper red (80—81).

By early afternoon of the next day we have reached the Euphrates (82—83). After the two-day journey through the desert this meeting with the mighty river is unusually impressive. Photograph 82 shows only a branch of the Euphrates, so shallow that one can easily wade across it. A small "water-lift" shows the kind of engineering that is employed in cultivating the land (83). On the horizontal shaft at the edge of the river bank there is a scoop wheel or Persian wheel which pulls up water in a constant stream when the whole contrivance is in operation. A simple toothed-wheel system converts the motion from the vertical axis to the horizontal. Careful irrigation makes possible the extensive cotton plantations laid out here.

82 Branch of the Euphrates
at Deir ez Zor

The photographs were taken in Deir ez Zor. Farther downstream is Dura-Europos, which rises sheer above the bank of the Euphrates. The right edge of our photograph (84) shows the wall of the citadel. The city area adjoins it on the west. Dura-Europos was not actually an "important" city, but it was significant because of its location and it played its part successively as a Seleucid fortress, a Parthian caravan city, and a Roman frontier garrison. It has been compared with Pompeii, which also was not an important city; in Dura-Europos as in Pompeii we have discovered unusually well-preserved remains of a small city. I have space to mention only two finds. First the Jewish synagogue excavated at Dura in 1932, in which the surprise was well-preserved colored wall frescoes. Its interior, partially reconstructed, can now be seen in the museum of Damascus. The wall paintings present scenes from the Old Testament, such as

83   Water-Lift on the Euphrates

Abraham, the exodus from Egypt and the wanderings in the desert, incidents from the time of the kings, the Elijah story, the destruction of Jerusalem in 587 B.C., and the book of Esther. Executed around 250 A.D., they are related in style and technique to other examples of the art of Dura. Also discovered in Dura was a somewhat earlier Christian church, actually a chapel built later into a private house, of the first century after Christ. This too was decorated with frescoes depicting biblical figures and stories, — Adam and Eve, David and Goliath, and from the Gospels the Good Shepherd, the Healing of the Paralytic, the Samaritan woman at Jacob's well, etc.

A little farther south the royal city of Mari was discovered in the rubble of Tell Hariri. Rich finds of texts here have illuminated the history of the early second century before Christ. More than 20,000 clay tablets give

84 View of the Euphrates
at Dura-Europos

us new insights into the political and economic situation and also make possible a more accurate dating of events and names already known. Commercial relations extended all the way to the Phoenician coast. The palace of the king was a famous sight in its own time and we too stand in amazement before its ruins. In the center were audience chambers and

85 Aleppo: Citadel

a throne room adorned with colored frescoes, and around it were great

courts. The palace structure contained more than three hundred rooms

for administrative offices and the archives, the court personnel and the

royal family. Among the finds was a table service consisting of nearly

fifty pieces. Mari was destroyed and dismantled around 1760 B.C. by the

86 Aleppo:
View from a Window oft the Citadel

128

famous Hammurabi of Babylon (who, according to the most recent dating,

reigned from 1793 to 1750 B.C. This was the end of Mari's rivalry. We

now return to the Mediterranean, keeping in general the course of the

northern caravan route, at first upstream on the Euphrates, until we turn

westward at Meskene and arrive at the Mediterranean coast by way of

Aleppo. We climb up to the citadel of Aleppo, which rises high above Syria's greatest city, a masterly example of the medieval Arabian art of fortification (85). Looking out of two different windows (86—87) we get a view of the city from above. In the picture on the left is a mosque with its pale blue cupolas in the immediate vicinity of the citadel. On the right the afternonn sun falls upon the great sea of houses in the city.

Herodotus said that Egypt was "the gift of the river," and a note by Pliny explains this by saying that hunger and plenty lie in the difference between twelve and sixteen ells of water level in the Nile. Therein lies a key to the economic problem of Egypt which is still applicable today. If one excludes the Nile delta between the Mediterranean coast and Cairo, Egypt is merely a narrow strip. Only on the banks of the river, as far as the turbid water of the Nile reaches by flooding and irrigation, is there any fertile black soil. Right next to it begins the red sand of the desert. All along its length it is possible to see the usable land on either side. Driving from Aswan to Cairo (between these two points the Nile extends almost 620 miles!), the traveler remains within sight of the edge of the desert, though the width of the cultivated land varies. It may be as narrow as five-eighths of a mile (at Aswan) and stretch out to twelve miles (at Cairo).

Very early Lower and Upper Egypt were distinguished as the "two lands." Lower Egypt is oriented toward the Mediterranean and its countries, whereas in Upper Egypt the trade runs to the south. Thus Upper Egypt is self-contained in a way quite different from the Delta area. We begin to understand, then, the role of Cairo and the ancient royal residence, Memphis, on the border between Lower and Upper Egypt, and the title "Lord of the Two Lands" assumed by the ancient Pharaohs. As is well

known, the symbol of the union of the two parts of the kingdom appears frequently in Egyptian art.

This brief reference to the geography of the country may be sufficient. The unique structure of the land explains why Egypt must make every effort not to allow a drop of the precious Nile water to go unused. So the rudimentary beginnings of irrigation by means of trenches and water wheels go back to very early times. Dams can retain and distribute over a longer period of time the floodwaters which come at the time of the thaw and the spring rains in the sources of the Blue Nile. They make possible more than one harvest a year. The new high dam Sadd el-Ali, four miles south of Aswan, is expected to increase the cultivable land by one and a half times. Incidentally, the old dam at Aswan was the largest in the world at the time it was built in the years 1898 to 1912.

88 Entering the Harbor of Alexandria

Here we are entering the harbor of Alexandria (88). Immediately below the horizon line one can see the harbor mole. A sailboat with slanted sail is crossing the path of the sun. This type of boat can be seen more clearly on photograph 89, the right edge of which shows the old Aswan dam.

89 Nile Boat at Aswan

Alexandria was founded by Alexander the Great; it was the first and also the most important of the many cities that owed their existence to him and his campaign to conquer the world. (Alexander was able to take Egypt without a battle.) Deinocrates, the architect of the city, carried out the royal plan with the lively co-operation of Alexander.

90 Isle of Philae: Kiosk

Five great city areas with broad, straight streets cutting each other at right angles arose on the site. The model for this kind of city planning was developed by the famous builder of cities, Hippodamus of Miletus. Alexander's great Macedonian general, the Diadochian Ptolemy I Soter (322–285), soon made Alexandria the capital city and laid the foundations for its rise as a world port and seat of culture. Here too was estab-

91 Entrance to the Temple of Isis:
Right Pylon

lished the renowned library in which was to be gathered the whole of Greek literature from Homer down to that time. Poets, painters, philologists, physicians, mathematicians, engineers, astronomers, and geographers of repute gathered in Alexandria. It was owing to the Hellenistic character of this city that here the Old Testament was translated into Greek (the so-called Septuagint) during the course of the third century before Christ.

I have emphasized this because we begin our picture sequence with the islet of Philae (south of Aswan), and the buildings of Philae definitely belong to the Ptolemaic period. It is true that the building of the temple of Isis extends beyond this time; it was begun under the last Dynasty

92 Temple of Isis: Four-Sided Hathor
    Capitals of the House of Birth

135

(the Thirtieth) and extended into the days of Trajan (98–117 A.D.). The influence of the Ptolemies was predominant, however. The "kiosk" is to be assigned to the time of the Roman Empire. Thus we are dealing here with relatively "recent" Egypt. The picturesque structure of the so-called "kiosk" with the rich variation of its flowered capitals is enchanting (90). Unfortunately, it was never finished. The upper blocks of the columns remain uncarved. They would have been given the form of four-sided Hathor capitals (cf. 92). Adjoining the kiosk is the chief temple of the island, the temple of Isis. Its walls and the shafts of the columns are covered with a network of hieroglyphic inscriptions and a great number of relief figures (91—92). At this time the hieroglyphs had actually become "hieroglyphs", in the sense of signs which could be read and interpreted only by a small circle of experts. We reach the outer court through an entrance which is flanked by pylons. At the top of the eastern pylon (91) two scenes are depicted. One of the Ptolemies stands before figures of gods, presenting the crown of Lower and Upper Egypt and making a sacrifice. Isis (on the left below) bears on her head the solar disk between two horns. During the Hellenistic era the cult of this originally Egyptian goddess spread throughout the Mediterranean world and far beyond. Isis became the "protean" goddess. A text from the second or third century after Christ (from Ios) is expressive of this concept:

"I am Isis, the sovereign of every land, and was reared by Hermes and with Hermes devised the demotic letters in order that everything might not be written in the same script. I gave the laws to men. . . . I am the eldest daughter of Cronos. I am the wife and the sister of Osiris the king. It is I who am called goddess by the women. I separated the earth from heaven. I gave the stars their courses. I ordered the path of the sun and the moon. I invented the trade of the seaman. . . . I brought woman and man together. . . . I gave the commandment that parents

should be loved by the children. ... I taught men to reverence the images of the gods. ... I instituted the dialect of the Hellenes and barbarians. ...''

The realtionship of the Ptolemies (including Alexander) to the Egyptian cults is to be seen in many different ways.

The four-sided Hathor capitals (92) are a part of the gallery of the ''house of birth'' on the west side of the outer court. Here Hathor-Isis is reverenced as the mother-goddess. Again we call attention to the varied forms of the shafts and capitals of the columns. The plant motifs occur in great ingenious variety on the ''bundle pillars'' and the capitals.

The fact that all the buildings on the islet are covered with a layer of brown mud is due to the Aswan dam. Only during a limited time in the year can one walk dry-shod on the island. However, the water level

93 Funerary Temple of Hatshepsut

137

toward the end of October was such that it was possible to go by boat to the interior of the temple of Isis.

■

Over 120 miles down the Nile is the ancient royal city which was called Thebes by the Greeks and now is called Luxor. Homer sang its praises: "Egyptian Thebes, which is the richest city in the whole world, for it has a hundred gates through each of which two hundred men may drive at once with their chariots and horses" (Il., IX, 382–384).

Homer's words still reflect the legendary splendor of the city from which once was ruled a world empire that stretched to the Euphrates and the Sudan. The "lords of the two lands" were bent upon becoming the masters of the world. Even today the abundance of monuments of a great past is overwhelming.

We begin with the funerary temple of Hatshepsut (1502–1481 B.C.), which is situated on the west bank of the Nile and boldly incorporated into the landscape (93). The 985-foot cliff and the temple structure, which originally had three colonnaded terraces, are bound together in a very convincing unity. The enormous background does not overwhelm the temple itself, but rather encloses it like a mighty frame and thus enhances its effect. Our picture also clearly shows the plan of the building with its ramps that lead from terrace to terrace.

Hatshepsut was the only woman ever to occupy the throne of the Pharaohs. She was the half-sister and wife of Thutmose II and after his death she seized control of the government. The gifted boy who was later to become Thutmose III was still very young. On the walls of her mortuary temple Hatshepsut boasted of no deeds of war. In the hall of Punt, however, a cycle of reliefs describes her economic and political expedition to the land of Punt (on the Somali coast). The initiative for this voyage is attributed to the god of Thebes, Amen-Re. "Her Majesty of the Palace made her entreaty at the steps of the Lord of the gods. From the great

138

throne was heard the command, an oracle of the god himself, to seek the way to Punt, to search the ways that lead to the slopes of the myrrh trees." The expedition proved to be a great succes and not unreasonably this is emphasized. Thus on the walls of the hall of Punt we see among other scenes the arrival and welcome of the Egyptian embassy, the reception of exchange goods, and the loading of the sailing ships for the return voyage. Chests of gold, ivory, myrrh trees, rare woods, and exotic animals are among the goods portrayed. The exactness of the artist's observation is striking. The representation of the fish, for example, is so faithful that it can be used to fix the geographical location of "Punt". "We feel as if we were looking at a manual of natural science" (W. Wolf). The expedition which King Solomon sent to Ophir over a half-century later presents a parallel on a smaller scale (I Kings

94 Colossi of Memnon

139

9–10). As we know, Solomon was interested in having a relationship with Egypt. He married an Egyptian princess (I Kings 3:1, 9:24, 11:1). A large part of the didactic literature is attributed to Solomon: "He . . . uttered three thousand proverbs; and his songs were a thousand and five" (I Kings 4:32) — and this proverbial literature is inconceivable apart from Egypt, where the art of the proverb was already an ancient one.

95 Tutankhamun
Wearing the Crown of Lower Egypt

140

Incidentally, Solomon, like Hatshepsut, appears not to have waged any wars.

Hatshepsut's style of government contrasts with that of her successor, Thutmose III. In a very short time it changed to an imperial policy of war. Another of the great Pharaohs was Amenophis III (1413–1375 B.C.). His tremendous activity as a builder extended as far as Nubia and the Sudan. He made a simple middle-class girl named Teye his queen, even though his origin might well have prompted him to be particularly careful about legitimacy. His father was of only half-royal birth and his mother was a Mitanni princess. Teye, however, was a noteworthy woman.

The power and wealth of the Pharaohs had grown to its greatest splendor at the time of Amenophis III, as is expressed in the so-called "Colossi

96 Mask of Tutankhamun

of Memnon" (94). These two immense seated figures, originally seventy feet high, stand at the entrance of the funerary temple of Amenophis III, of which nothing else remains. The tendency toward exaggerated dimensions which we have already noted in Rameses II is therefore older than Rameses. Each of these Amenophis figures was carved out of a single sandstone block. An earthquake did severe damage to the figure

97 Medinet Habu:
    Throne Room and Audience Window

142

on the right. These figures came to be called the Colossi of Memnon in the time of the Ptolemies, when the historical connections were no longer exactly known, though they were never completely forgotten. After the earthquake the right colossus gave forth a sound at dawn and this musical phenomenon, which has not been fully explained to this day, was interpreted as the greeting of Memnon, who according to legend

98 Medinet Habu: Philistine Prisoners

143

was born of Aurora, the goddess of dawn, addressed to his "rosy-fingered" mother. After the restoration of the figure around 200 A.D. the phenomenon disappeared.

After Amenophis III came his son Akhenaton (1375–1358 B.C.), who is so difficult to understand and so fragile-appearing compared with his vital, energetic father. His wife was the beautiful Nofretete. He made a name for himself as a reformer of the religious traditions. His transference of the royal residence to Amarna in Middle Egypt, which he undertook as part of his reformation, was temporary. The losses suffered by Egypt under Akhenaton in Syria and Palestine, and presumably in Africa too, were very great. This much is indicated in the letters of the royal archives of Āmarna, the so-called Tell el-Amarna tablets. Internally, there were severe political crises.

This encumbered heritage was taken over by the consort of a daughter of Akhenaton, the youthful Tutankhamun (1358–1350 B.C.). He returned to Thebes and restored the old traditions, but to restore Egypt's world power took some time. The renewed vigor of the empire began with the reign of the first bearer of the name Rameses or his son Seti I. But Egypt never succeeded fully in regaining its ancient power. Tutankhamun died young. His name is familiar to us because of the famous discovery of his tomb in the Valley of the Kings. We present here only a small indication of the rich treasures revealed in this hitherto unrobbed grave. In the museum at Cairo there is a gold-coated figure of the king, wearing the crown of Lower Egypt and standing upon a Nile bark in hunting attitude—a reminder of the great Pharaohs' love of the chase (95). The mask of beaten gold and lapis lazuli shows a vulture and serpent above and bears the features of the youthful king (96). This is unquestionably a masterpiece of the goldsmith's art.

Rameses II we have already met, on one of his advances to the north across the land bridge of Palestine–Syria (3). We showed the porphyry

head from the court of his funerary temple on the west bank of the Nile at Thebes (4). If we go south from this funerary temple, the so-called Rameseum, we come to Medinet Habu and the temple and palace of Rameses III (1198–1166 B.C.). The two buildings are closely connected. From the throne room of the Pharaoh we look over to the wall of the temple. When the Pharaoh was in residence here he could go through the passage in the wall directly to the "audience window" to show himself to the people assembled in the court of the temple (97). Typical is the representation of the Pharaoh to the right and the left of the passage. It is a symmetrical repetition of the same scene: with one hand the Pharaoh holds a "bundle" of prisoners by the hair while the other is drawn back ready to strike them with a cudgel. Another typical relief from Medinet Habu (98) shows Rameses again in the attitude of a victor, hold-

99 Luxor: Sunset

145

ing shackled prisoners by a cord. The bottom row of prisoners can be clearly identified. The helmet with feathered crest, and the so-called Greek profile with its straight line from a high forehead to the nose show them to be Philistines. Under Rameses III the Philistines were for the first time referred to as "Pulastu". They were a part of the Sea Peoples, who ever since the fourteenth century had been pressing in to the coastlands of the eastern Mediterranean: the Sardinians, Sicilians, Tyrsenians, Lycians, and Achaeans. After long struggles the Philistines were able to gain a foothold on the coastal plain of southern Palestine, where we find them in the Old Testament. Under David they were conquered. Whether their original home was in the Balkan Peninsula or the Aegadean Islands, we do not know.

What strikes us in this relief is the avoidance of conventionalized representation, which we might have expected, considering the subject. It is amazing how different from each other the heads of the Philistines are in expression and attitude. Here the "theme" was richly varied.

■

Thus, as our examples at least indicate, the history of Egypt can be illustrated to an unexpectedly great extent by the discoveries made in Luxor. In closing we look once more from the east bank to the west (99).

The three following photographs belong together (100—102). They give us a glimpse of the cultivation of the land along the Nile. We note that the living and working conditions of the Egyptian farmers have remained largely unchanged for thousands of years. We have already spoken of the importance that the Nile and its floods have for the country. Going by express from Luxor to Cairo (the pictures were taken from the moving train), one receives some very direct visual instruction in how the water is distributed and what the soil looks like before the land is cultivated (100). In the next photograph the planting and cultivation have already begun and the ground is covered with the first shoots of

green. In the foreground a farmer is wading through a broad canal. Quite close to the fields are the villages with their simple clay cottages between tall palm trees (101). Then last a very instructive scene: whole crews of agricultural laborers at work (101). Who is not reminded here of the beginnings of Israel's history and the sojourn of the tribes in Egypt? The photograph with which the book closes confronts us with Egypt at its most ancient. It shows the "step pyramid" of King Djoser at Saqqara (103). The famous pyramids of Giza are higher and better known. When Napoleon stood at the foot of the Great Pyramid (that of Cheops or Khufu), he calculated that its cubic content would be sufficient to surround all of France with a wall over nine feet high. Our step pyramid, however, is the earliest of the pyramids. The time of King Djoser's reign is now set at 2632–2613 B.C. Only meager remains of the ancient capi-

100 Nile: Flood Plain

147

tal Memphis have survived. But as one looks to the west from the site of
ancient Memphis one sees not far away the pyramid of Djoser, which in
the course of its construction grew with its six steps to a height of
197 feet. This contains the tomb of the king. The fact that it lies in the west
is not accidental. For the Egyptians the land of the dead lay in the direction of the setting sun. We know the name of the architect who constructed the pyramid with such admirable engineering precision: Im-
hotep. He also put his stamp upon the beginnings of the ancient kingdom in other respects.

The foundations at Saqqara (there are other buildings besides the pyramid) are an early sign of the power and rigid concentration of the Egyptian state in the hands of the ruler, who had at his command all officials
and all the people.

101 Beginning of Cultivation

In the last pages we have gone far beyond the narrower confines of biblical history. The time of Egypt's greatest power antedated the beginning of the Israelite tribes' invasion of Palestine. Ever new powers kept pushing themselves into the foreground in the course of history. Empires came and went. We have been able only to touch lightly upon the notable movements that took place in the ancient Middle East, but even so it is apparent that the history told by the Bible is interwoven with them all.

This does not mean that Israel played an important political role among its powerful neighbors. After Solomon's death the great kingdom of David which Solomon inherited disintegrated into its parts "almost overnight" (Albrecht Alt). Thus that empire was really an exception in Israel's history. In general Israel made history less than it suffered history. What

102   Fellahin at Work in the Fields

149

makes Israel unique cannot be measured by the standard of world history. Nor is it to be found in what Israel itself was, in some possible hidden superiority that made it more excellent than other nations. If you look at it this way, you will be missing the very thing that made Israel Israel, even if you see its superiority as being a religious accomplishment. What constitutes the singularity of Israel, beyond any glory that Israel might have of itself, is the unfathomable act of God in turning to and choosing Israel:

"The Lord your God has chosen you to be a people for his own possession, out of all the peoples that are on the face of the earth."

This is the central thing; but then the biblical text goes on to say in unmistakable terms what it means:

"It was not because you were more in number than any other people that the Lord set his love upon you and chose you, for you were the fewest of all peoples; but it is because the Lord loves you, and is keeping the oath which he swore to your fathers, that the Lord has brought you out with a mighty hand, and redeemed you from the house of bondage, from the hand of Pharaoh king of Egypt" (Deut. 7:6–8).

Or we may find what is the substance of the history of Israel stated with a similar insistence in the words of the Second Isaiah:
"But now thus says the Lord, he who created you, O Jacob,

he who formed you, O Israel;
'Fear not, for I have redeemed you;

I have called you by name, you are mine.
When you pass through the waters I will be with you;

and through the rivers, they shall not overwhelm you;
When you walk through fire you shall not be burned,

and the flame shall not consume you.
For I am the Lord your God, the Holy One of Israel, your Savior.
I give Egypt as your ransom, Ethiopia and Seba in exchange for you.

Because you are precious in my eyes,

    and honored, and I love you,

I give men in return for you,

    peoples in exchange for your life.'" (Isa. 43:1–4)

This tells us what makes Israel Israel: the incomparable wonder of the elective love of God. This is the "royal" theme of its history, even though Israel itself often fails to recognize it. Knowing that theme, we hold Israel's history no far-off thing, but history that is near to us, just as surely as Israel's God is the God of all the world. Knowing this theme, we know that Israel's history is not a triumphal march in the midst of world history, but rather the story of God's meeting with his people.

103   Step Pyramid at Saqqara

LIST OF THE PHOTOGRAPHS

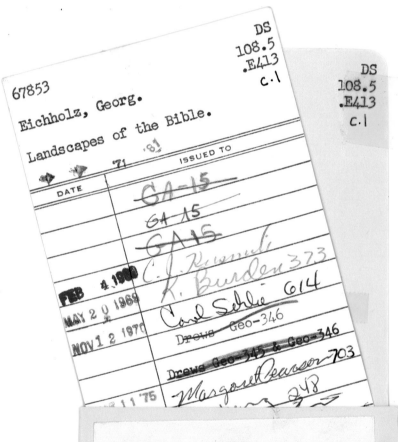

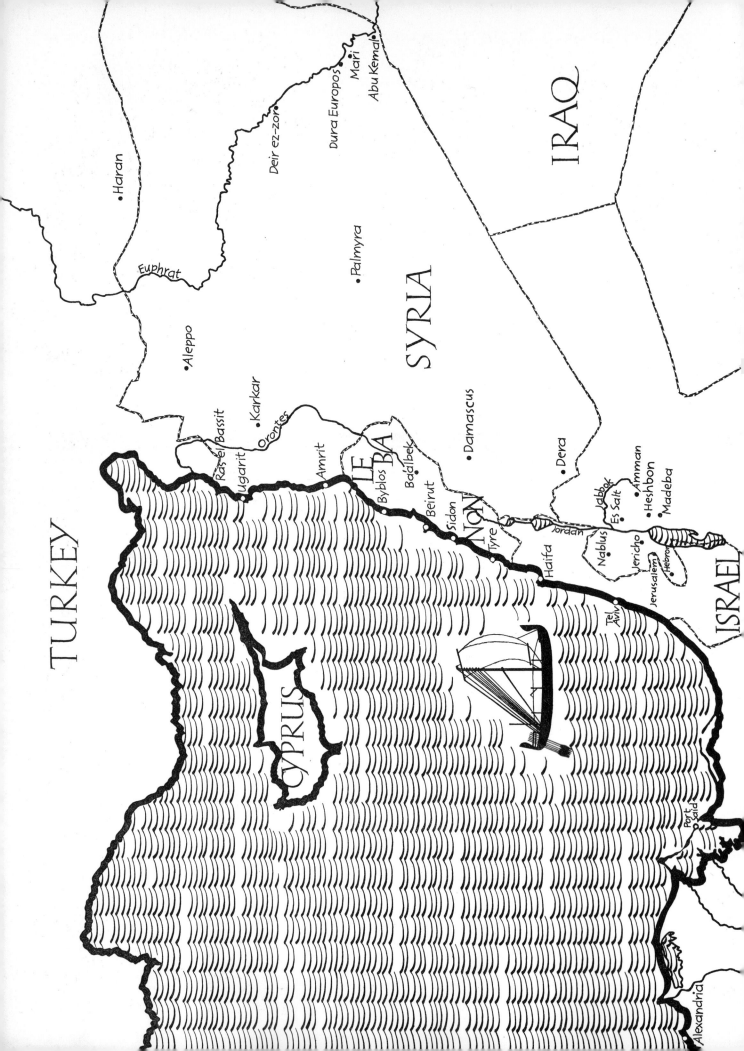

TURKEY

•Haran

Euphrat

Deir ez-zor•

Dura Europos•
Mari•
Abu Kemal•

IRAQ

•Palmyra

SYRIA

Aleppo•

Ras el Bassit
•Karkar
Ugarit• Orontes

Amrit•

LE BA
Byblos•
Báalbek•
Beirut•
Sidon•
NON
Tyre•

•Damascus

•Dera

Jabbok
•Amman
Es Salt •Heshbon
Madeba

Haifa•

Nablus•
Jericho•
Jerusalem•
•Hebron

Jordan

Tel
Aviv•

ISRAEL

CYPRUS

Port
Said

Alexandria